CAMBRIDGE LIBRARY COLLECTION

Books of enduring scholarly value

Religion

For centuries, scripture and theology were the focus of prodigious amounts of scholarship and publishing, dominated in the English-speaking world by the work of Protestant Christians. Enlightenment philosophy and science, anthropology, ethnology and the colonial experience all brought new perspectives, lively debates and heated controversies to the study of religion and its role in the world, many of which continue to this day. This series explores the editing and interpretation of religious texts, the history of religious ideas and institutions, and not least the encounter between religion and science.

Prolegomena to St Paul's Epistles to the Romans and the Ephesians

This posthumous volume, published in 1895, contains two lectures delivered in the 1880s by the biblical scholar F. J. A. Hort, Professor of Divinity at Cambridge. In these lectures, Hort addresses the question of the dating of Romans and Ephesians, their purpose, and their original readership. He examines their context in the relationship of Judaism to Christianity in the Apostolic period and the difference between Gentile, Judaistic and Roman Christianity. By treating the Epistles as historical as well as religious artefacts and analysing their language and grammar as well as content, Hort argues for the authenticity of both texts and therefore for a first-century dating. The dating of the New Testament was a central concern of Hort toward the end of his career, and he argued against F. C. Baur and the Tübingen school, who placed it in the second century. These lectures present evidence to support his argument.

T0382513

Cambridge University Press has long been a pioneer in the reissuing of out-of-print titles from its own backlist, producing digital reprints of books that are still sought after by scholars and students but could not be reprinted economically using traditional technology. The Cambridge Library Collection extends this activity to a wider range of books which are still of importance to researchers and professionals, either for the source material they contain, or as landmarks in the history of their academic discipline.

Drawing from the world-renowned collections in the Cambridge University Library, and guided by the advice of experts in each subject area, Cambridge University Press is using state-of-the-art scanning machines in its own Printing House to capture the content of each book selected for inclusion. The files are processed to give a consistently clear, crisp image, and the books finished to the high quality standard for which the Press is recognised around the world. The latest print-on-demand technology ensures that the books will remain available indefinitely, and that orders for single or multiple copies can quickly be supplied.

The Cambridge Library Collection will bring back to life books of enduring scholarly value (including out-of-copyright works originally issued by other publishers) across a wide range of disciplines in the humanities and social sciences and in science and technology.

Prolegomena to St Paul's Epistles to the Romans and the Ephesians

FENTON JOHN ANTHONY HORT

CAMBRIDGE
UNIVERSITY PRESS

CAMBRIDGE UNIVERSITY PRESS

Cambridge, New York, Melbourne, Madrid, Cape Town, Singapore,
São Paolo, Delhi, Dubai, Tokyo

Published in the United States of America by Cambridge University Press, New York

www.cambridge.org
Information on this title: www.cambridge.org/9781108007511

© in this compilation Cambridge University Press 2009

This edition first published 1895
This digitally printed version 2009

ISBN 978-1-108-00751-1 Paperback

PROLEGOMENA

TO ST PAUL'S EPISTLES TO

THE ROMANS AND THE EPHESIANS

PROLEGOMENA

TO ST PAUL'S EPISTLES TO

THE ROMANS
AND THE EPHESIANS

BY THE LATE

F. J. A. HORT, D.D., D.C.L., LL.D.,

LADY MARGARET PROFESSOR OF DIVINITY
IN THE UNIVERSITY OF CAMBRIDGE

London

MACMILLAN AND CO.

AND NEW YORK

1895

NOTE.

THESE Lectures introductory to the Epistles to the Romans and Ephesians are published with the fewest possible variations from the manuscript of the Lectures as delivered. It will be obvious that they do not cover the whole ground, as laid out by Dr Hort. But so far as they go, they clearly form an invaluable contribution to the study of those Epistles. This will justify their publication in their fragmentary condition.

The task of editing has been confined to the verification of quotations and the supply of headings to the pages and chapters. These have been framed as closely as possible on the phraseology of the text itself.

It is hoped that some specimens of commentary on these Epistles may be published with other Adversaria in another volume.

Easter, 1895.

CONTENTS.

INTRODUCTION

TO THE

EPISTLE TO THE ROMANS

THE EPISTLE TO THE ROMANS.

[*EASTER TERM*, 1886.]

I PROPOSE this term to lecture on the Epistle to
the Romans, in itself an enormous subject. To deal
properly with it would need not merely a longer term
than this, but many terms. Even however in this
unusually short term I hope that by rigorous
selection of topics we may be able to get some
substantial hold of the Epistle; and, owing to the
peculiar position which it holds among St Paul's
Epistles, even a very imperfect study of it will yield
more instruction than a somewhat less imperfect
study of, I believe we may say, any other single
Epistle of St Paul would have done.

In this case, perhaps more than usual, the benefit
to be derived from attending lectures must be pro-
portional to the time and care spent upon the subject
by members of the class in private work. The
utmost that a lecturer can do is to supply suggestions
which can be verified and followed up at home.

One question that often has to be discussed can here be dismissed at once—that of the authorship.   There is practically no dispute among different schools (unless it be in Holland) that St Paul wrote this Epistle, or at least the greater part of it : some would except the last chapter, or the last two : but the bulk of the Epistle may be treated as confessedly written by the Apostle whose name it bears.   So also as to its readers : no one doubts that they were Romans and Roman Christians.   On the other hand there has been and is much discussion whether these Roman Christians were exclusively Jewish Christians, or exclusively Gentile Christians, or both the one and the other ; and this question is connected with another as to the origin of the Roman Church, and its characteristics at the time when St Paul wrote.

The fifteenth chapter, if part of the original Epistle, fixes the date at a glance : but even in its absence there is hardly room for doubt.   The Epistle, that is, was written at Corinth towards the close of what is called St Paul's Third Missionary Journey, shortly before he sailed for Jerusalem to make the visit which led to that long imprisonment described in the later chapters of the Acts.   According to the reckoning now most generally received, this would be in the spring of the year 58, or possibly the preceding winter, when Nero had just completed the third year of his reign.   This absolute or numerical date is however of less consequence than the relative date, that is, the place of the Epistle in St Paul's writings, and its place in his life.

The purpose of the Epistle must next be considered. Was it simply polemical? Was it an abstract and as it were independent dogmatic treatise? Had it any further special intention? These questions take us into the heart of the Epistle itself, and lead the way to a consideration of its plan and structure. That the problem is not very simple or easy may be reasonably inferred from the extraordinary variety of opinion which has prevailed and still prevails about it. But it is worthy of any pains that can be taken for its solution; for so long as the purpose of the Epistle remains obscure, the main drift of its doctrinal teaching must remain obscure also; and though there is much Apostolic Christianity which is not expressly set forth in the Epistle to the Romans, yet that Epistle holds such a place among the authoritative documents of the faith, that any grave misunderstanding respecting it is likely to lead to misunderstanding of Apostolic Christianity. If we look back on the history of doctrine, we can see that in the case of this Epistle, as of all the larger writings of the New Testament, there are considerable elements which have never yet been duly recognised and appropriated. But it is equally true that portions of the Epistle to the Romans have had an enormous influence on theological thought. In conjunction with the preparatory Epistle to the Galatians this Epistle is the primary source of Augustinian Theology, itself renewing its strength from time to time, and more especially in various shapes in the age of the Reformation. We have therefore every reason for trying to gain the most comprehensive view that we can of what St Paul really meant, and in so doing I think we shall find that, as usual, the worst stumbling blocks belong not to the Apostolic teaching itself but to arbitrary limitations of it.

The various points which we have seen to require discussion under the head of Introduction are all closely connected together; so closely that some repetitions will be unavoidable. But for the sake of clearness they must be considered separately.

I.

THE ROMAN CHURCH.

A.

*INFORMATION FROM THE NEW TESTAMENT
GENERALLY.*

FIRST, the Roman Church and its origin. At the
outset we have to notice the prominent negative fact
that it had never been visited by St Paul; much less
had it been founded by him. We shall have to return
to this fact presently to bring out its influence on St
Paul's thoughts in connexion with the purpose of the
Epistle: but for the moment it concerns us only as
affecting the Romans themselves. Neither here nor
anywhere else in the New Testament have we the
smallest hint as to the origin of this great Church;
and practically we are left to conjecture respecting it.
After a while indeed it was said that St Peter was the
founder. He was represented as the first bishop of
Rome, and was assigned an episcopate of twenty-five
or twenty years, reaching back almost to the beginning
of the reign of Claudius. Possibly, as has been suggested, this date may be due to a combination of the
statement of Justin[1], repeated by Irenæus, that Simon

[1] Justin M. *Apol.* i. 26; Iren. i. 23. 1 (ed. Stieren).

Magus was worshipped at Rome in the time of Claudius, with the tradition[1] that St Peter encountered Simon Magus at Rome.   However this may be, the whole story of St Peter's early connexion with Rome is a manifest error or fiction; and all that we know on good authority respecting the early spread of the Gospel is adverse to the belief that the Roman Church was founded by any apostle or envoy of the apostles; nor is it likely that had such been the case there would have been no trace of it in the Epistle itself. St Paul's own progress towards the work was quite tentative.   It was only the vision of the man of Macedonia that brought him over into Europe in the first instance.   When he wrote the fifteenth chapter his labours had extended as far as Illyricum, but still on the Eastern side of the Hadriatic, and there is no sign that he deliberately sent pioneers before him. But when he wrote, the Roman Church cannot have been of recent foundation, for he had himself been for some considerable number of years desiring to see it.   Hardly more than six years seem to have passed since he had first entered Europe: so that the foundation of the Church must in all probability have taken place in an earlier state of things.

How early, it is impossible to say.   The intercourse between the great Jewish community at Rome and the mother city Jerusalem must have provided a

Acts xvi. 9.

Rom. xv. 19.

Rom. xv. 23.

---

[1] Euseb. *H. E.* ii. 14; Hippolytus, *Ref. Haer.* vi. 20: cf. Lightfoot, *Clement*, vol. ii. p. 491 (ed. 1890).

channel by which the Christian message might be carried to Rome in the first years after the Ascension. The allusion to Roman sojourners at Jerusalem as present on the first Christian Day of Pentecost Acts ii. 10. is a confirmation from the New Testament of what is sufficiently attested from other sources. But whether as a matter of fact the Christian faith did make its way to Rome during that period is more than we can tell. The story of Clement, as told in both the extant forms of the Clementine romance[1], makes Barnabas bring the Gospel to Rome as early as the reign of Tiberius: but this is a mere fable, probably originating towards the end of the second century. It was probably by a process of quiet and as it were fortuitous filtration that the Roman Church was formed; and the process is more likely to have repeated itself on different occasions than to have taken place once for all. An obscure and gradual origin best suits the manner of St Paul's language. Andronicus and Junia (or Junias), St Rom. xvi. Paul's kinsmen and fellow prisoners, are said to [7.] have been Christians before his conversion: but we cannot tell whether they originally belonged to Rome, or took up their abode there at some later time. We are on somewhat firmer ground in respect of Aquila and Prisca (or Priscilla), who stand at the head of the persons saluted in the sixteenth chapter,

[1] *Clementine Homilies*, i. 9, *Recognitions*, i. 6, 7 (Cotelier, *Patres Apostolici*, 1700).

and are mentioned in very emphatic terms. Aquila
was a Jew, by birth a native of Pontus (i.e. probably
Sinope, like the later Aquila the translator), and apparently settled at Rome. He first comes before us
as having left Italy with his wife Priscilla because
Claudius had decreed that all the Jews should depart
from Rome, and having come to Corinth shortly
before St Paul went there from Athens. St Luke
does not give the least intimation as to the time
when Aquila and Priscilla became Christians. On the
whole it seems most probable that their conversion
preceded their acquaintance with St Paul, and that
they had felt Claudius' decree to be as hostile to their
stay at Rome as it was to that of unbelieving Jews.
It is difficult otherwise to see how St Paul could have
at once joined himself to them, and wrought with
Aquila at the same employment, as the very next
verse describes. Twice more in the same chapter we
hear of them, and then they disappear from the Acts.
They accompany St Paul to Ephesus when he leaves
Corinth, and at Ephesus they correct and enlarge
Apollos' imperfect knowledge of Christian doctrine.
They are either *still* at Ephesus or *again* at Ephesus
about three years later, when the first Epistle to the
Corinthians was written, and at a much later time
they are once more at Ephesus when the second
Epistle to Timothy was written. In the interval, a
little less than a year after the writing of the first
Epistle to the Corinthians, comes this reference in the

Acts xviii. 2.

Acts xviii. 18.
Acts xviii. 26.

1 Cor. xvi. 19.

2 Tim. iv. 19.

sixteenth chapter of the Epistle to the Romans, which
harmonises with St Luke's original account, for it
was natural enough that Aquila and Priscilla should
return to Rome when it had become safe to do so.
If Rome had not been their usual place of residence,
but they had merely paid it a passing visit, it is not
likely that St Luke would have gone out of his way
to speak of the edict of Claudius, in order to account
for their being at Corinth when St Paul went there.
It is of course equally clear that they were much at
Ephesus. We should probably understand their
movements better if we knew more about the
occupation which Aquila and St Paul alike followed,
that of σκηνοποιοί, probably rightly translated 'tent- Acts xviii.
makers'; most of what is found on the subject in ³·
modern books being pure guess-work, with hardly
any foundation of ancient evidence. It is likely
enough that St Paul's special interest in the Christian
community at Rome, though hardly perhaps his
knowledge of it, dates from his acquaintance with
Aquila and Priscilla at Corinth. This was somewhere
about six years before the writing of the Epistle to
the Romans, and that interval would perhaps suffice
to justify his language about having desired to visit
them ἀπὸ ἱκανῶν ἐτῶν (a rather vague phrase, not so Rom. xv.
strong as the ἀπὸ πολλῶν ἐτῶν which was easily sub- ²³·
stituted for it). There is nothing to shew that Aquila
and Priscilla were in any sense the founders of the
Roman Church: about that we know nothing: but

the position which they hold in the sixteenth chapter of our Epistle could hardly have been given them if their position in the Roman Church itself had not been a specially prominent one, even as it was in St Paul's own previous thoughts about the Roman Church.

In this connexion a suggestion made by Dean Plumptre in a paper on Aquila and Priscilla in his ingenious and interesting 'Biblical Studies' deserves special attention. It has often been noticed that the wife Prisca is named before the husband Aquila in four out of the six places where both are named: the fifth passage is no instance to the contrary, on account of the structure of the sentence: the only true exception is in the first Epistle to the Corinthians. It has been the fashion to suppose that Prisca was given this precedence on account of her higher zeal or devotion, of which however the Bible tells us nothing. Dr Plumptre suggests with much greater probability that she was a Roman lady, of higher rank than her husband, and that her position in Rome enabled her to render special services to the Church. On this point St Luke's testimony is simply neutral. He does not say that Priscilla was a Jewess, as is often assumed, or that she was of Pontus: these statements are made of Aquila alone, and then it is added that on his departure from Italy he was accompanied by his wife. Her name with St Paul (according to the true text) is always Prisca, with St Luke Priscilla:

[margin notes:] Acts xviii. 18, 26. Rom. xvi. 3. 2 Tim. iv. 19. Acts xviii. 2. 1 Cor. xvi. 19.

both forms were doubtless in use. Dr Plumptre justly observes that Priscus was an illustrious and ancient Roman name; and it may be added that it was borne by many in the age of St Paul. Prisca may of course have been of servile or libertine origin, and derived her name from the household to which she belonged: but it may also have been her own family name. The supposition here made agrees with other known facts. There is good reason to believe that the *superstitio externa* for which " Pomponia Graecina insignis femina[1]" was accused about the time when the Epistle to the Romans was written was the Christian faith; and the same is true of the charge on which Domitian's cousins, Flavius Clemens and his wife Flavia Domitilla, were condemned[2].

Another coincidence corroborative of Dr Plumptre's suggestion seems to have escaped his notice. Within the last few years it has become clear that during the ages of persecution the Christians at Rome derived great help from immunities connected with cemeteries which they were practically able to use as their own, and that this free use of cemeteries chiefly came to them through the connexion of the cemeteries with important Roman families in which Christians had gained adherents.

[1] Tac. *Ann.* xiii. 32, cf. Lightfoot, *Philippians*, p. 21 (4th edition), *Clement*, i. p. 31 ff. (ed. 1890).

[2] Lightfoot, *Phil.* p. 21 ff. (4th edition). *Clement*, i. pp. 33 ff. (ed. 1890).

Thus one, which was called the *Coemeterium Do-mitillae*, has been shown with great probability to have belonged to this very Flavia Domitilla who was banished as a Christian[1]. Now another cemetery, or (to use the popular word) 'catacomb', bearing marks that, in the opinion of the best judges, shew it to be one of the most ancient of all, probably dating from the first century[2], was known from a very early time as the Coemeterium Priscillae. The Roman traditions contain no reference to the name as belonging to the cemetery: but it seems likely enough that it came from the wife of Aquila. One tradition of no authority in itself, makes the cemetery to have belonged to Pudens[3], 2 Tim. iv. named in the second Epistle to Timothy; and 21. another makes Priscilla to be the mother of Pudens[4]. Thus indirectly tradition, *valeat quantum*, affords some confirmation of a supposition which has been suggested by other considerations.

If such was the social position of Prisca or Priscilla, fresh light is thrown thereby on the prominence given to both her and her husband in the sixteenth chapter of this Epistle, and on their special fitness for being the chief connecting link

---

[1] Lightfoot, *Clement*, i. p. 35 ff. (1890).

[2] Kraus, *Roma Sott.* 71 f., 384 f., 540 (2nd edition, 1879); *Real-Encycl.* ii. 108 *b*.

[3] Kraus, *R.E.* l.c., cf. *R. Sott.* 71.

[4] Kraus, *R. Sott.* 549.

between St Paul and the Roman Church before he visited Rome himself.

Next, these relations between St Paul and Aquila and Priscilla have an important bearing on the much debated question as to the nature of the Christianity which prevailed among the Roman Christians. But first we must look back a little. If the new faith was carried direct to Rome at a very early time, say before the preaching of St Stephen, it would naturally bear the stamp of Palestine and be marked by the limitations of a state of things in which the transitory nature of Judaism was not yet clearly recognised. If however some time had passed before the Gospel reached Rome, or if it arrived there not direct from Palestine but through some intermediate channel, Jewish characteristics are likely to have been, at least, less strongly impressed upon it : such would be the natural result alike of the general influence of the Jews of the Dispersion, and of the Hellenistic movement at Jerusalem itself which we associate with the name of St Stephen. Nay even if the earliest Roman Christianity was of a strictly Judaic type, there was no reason why it should not in due time be modified by the influence of the progress which was going on in the East, provided that the communications with the Christians of the East were continued or renewed : we have no right to call it unnatural either that the old characteristics should be stiffly maintained, or that they should gradually yield to new influences. Again, a third state of things took its beginning when St Paul went forth from Antioch to preach the Gospel to the heathen. From this time forward the labours of St Paul himself and his associates, first in Asia Minor and then in Macedonia and Greece, must have started many little waves, as it were, of Christian movement, some of which could hardly fail to reach as far as Rome. The Christianity they carried would as a matter of course be the Christianity of St Paul himself, so far as it was understood by the bearers of it : and, as in the former supposed case, if it found at Rome a pre-existing Christianity of more Jewish type, the old might either pass into the new or remain unchanged. There was no necessity or likelihood that any violent antagonism should arise between them, unless a fresh element should be introduced in the shape of Jewish emissaries deliberately sent from the East to counterwork St Paul. Such would certainly be a possible contingency : but what evidence we have is not favourable to it. The words spoken to St Paul by the Jews at Rome in the last chapter of Acts xxviii. the Acts, the genuineness of which I cannot see any 21, 22. sufficient reason to doubt, render it virtually incredible that only a few years before attempts had been made at Rome to oppose St Paul and his Gospel in the Jewish interest.

But at this point his relations with Aquila and Prisca come in with special force. Their close association with St Paul would of itself have been almost decisive for the Pauline character of their Christianity. But it so happens that the chapter of the Acts which first introduces them exhibits them also at Ephesus in a light which leaves no room Acts xviii. 26. for doubt. It was as a Christian that Apollos came to Ephesus (he had been κατηχημένος τὴν ὁδὸν τοῦ Κυρίου), and ἐδίδασκεν ἀκριβῶς τὰ περὶ τοῦ Ἰησοῦ, while he was familiar (ἐπιστάμενος) with the baptism of John only : and this imperfection in his knowledge of the faith, however we may understand the terms in which it is described, was corrected by Aquila and Prisca, who expounded to him the way of God more exactly (ἀκριβέστερον). It is incredible that St Luke would have used this language if their own belief had fallen short of the standard of growth represented by St Paul's Gospel. Now it would not be safe to argue backwards from this fact to the time when Aquila and Prisca were at Rome before they knew St Paul. Their Christianity at that time, on the assumption that they were at that time Christians, might be either Pauline or not, for doubtless intercourse with St Paul at Corinth during that year and a half would have sufficed to bring them to his point of view if they did not occupy it already. But we may safely draw a conclusion as to the time subsequent to that intercourse at Corinth. The Christianity which they maintained in person at Rome when they were there, and which they encouraged in others at Rome with whom they held communications when themselves at

Ephesus or elsewhere at a distance, must, we may be sure, have been such as St Paul would have approved. This does not exclude the possibility that older and cruder forms of the faith still survived at Rome: it does exclude the supposition that the Epistle was intended to introduce a new doctrine hitherto strange to the Roman Christians.

This is all, I believe, that can be safely laid down respecting the probable or possible conditions under which the Church of Rome was founded, and under which it had lived up to the time when St Paul's Epistle was written. As regards the nature of Roman Christianity at that time, looking for the moment exclusively at these probabilities as to the origin and history of the Roman Church, and at the relations in which Prisca and Aquila stood to St Paul on the one hand and to the Roman Church on the other, we first find reason to believe, that Pauline Christianity had at least a firm footing there and not, apparently, on hostile terms; and next, it is probable, rather on general grounds than on definite historical evidence, that Jewish types of Christianity, one or more, had likewise their representatives.

THE ROMAN CHURCH.

B.

INTERNAL EVIDENCE OF THE EPISTLE.

WE must now give a little attention to the evidence, as to the character of the Roman Church, which the Epistle itself contains, partly in its language, partly in such inferences as we may be able to draw from peculiarities and limitations in the subjects which it treats and the arguments which it uses. Critical discussion of the problem has run through a curious history, into the minute details of which however it would take us too long to enter. The old view, suggested by certain conspicuous phrases, was that the Epistle was addressed to heathen converts. Nearly half a century ago a complete change was brought about by one of the most brilliant and most perverse of critics, Ferdinand Baur. He rendered a great service to the criticism of this as of other books of the New Testament by insisting strongly on the need of reading it in connexion with the movements and controversies of the age in which it was written : but unfortunately his own view of the Apostolic Age was full of exaggeration and distortion ; and thus the

misreading of history produced a misreading of literature, which for the moment undid the salutary effects
of reading history and literature together. Hence the
Roman Church addressed in the Epistle was declared
to be a Church of Jewish Christians. This paradox
was for many years accepted by leading critics of
very different schools, though sometimes with more or
less modification and dilution. Ten years ago however an essay by another great critic, Weizsäcker[1],
caused an important reaction. The error introduced
through an appeal to external history was corrected
through an appeal to a better understanding of external history. It was urged that there was no ground
for assuming, as practically was done, that all Christians of that date were members either of a definitely
Pauline party, or of a definitely Judaizing party hostile
to St Paul and his doctrines. It was more reasonable
to suppose that multitudes of Christians occupied a
virtually neutral ground, neither following the stricter
precepts of the Jewish Law, nor making it a matter of
principle to treat the Law as no longer binding. The
existence of large bodies of Christians of such a type
was a natural consequence of the fact that the communities of Jews and strict proselytes were surrounded
by large numbers of what we may call semi-proselytes,
men whose faith was the Jewish faith, but who adopted
Jewish observances to a limited extent only.

During the last ten years this idea of the Roman

[1] [*Jahrbuch für deutsche Theologie*, 1876, p. 248 f.]

Church as largely of Gentile origin has been constantly gaining ground. It is now agreed virtually on all hands that it cannot have been either exclusively Jewish or exclusively Gentile. The differences of opinion which still exist are chiefly as to the proportion borne by the one element to the other, and as to the nature of the relations between the two elements presumed to have given rise to St Paul's arguments directed against the permanence of Judaism.

It has been said that the language of the Epistle to the Romans presupposes Gentile readers, and its substance Jewish readers. The meaning of this exaggerative paradox is that St Paul repeatedly uses the term ἔθνη as, apparently, applicable to his readers, while a large part of his argument is intended to convince men disposed to believe that the Jewish Law was meant to be permanently binding. It is worth while to glance at some of the passages which contain the former class of evidence: the arguments which form the other class are too obvious to need pointing out. In the opening salutation, St Paul speaks of Rom. i. 5, having received grace and apostleship ἐν πᾶσιν τοῖς ⁶· ἔθνεσιν, 'among whom are ye also, called of Jesus Christ.' Here the interpretation of ἔθνεσιν as a geographical, not a religious term, i.e. as meaning nations, including the Jewish people, not nations as opposed to it, makes ἐν οἷς ἐστε καὶ ὑμεῖς a peculiarly bald and flat mode of expression: yet this is the only way to escape the inference that the men addressed were

Gentiles. So also in *v.* 13 of the same chapter, ' that I may have some fruit in you also as also ἐν τοῖς λοιποῖς ἔθνεσιν', the Romans are as distinctly called ἔθνη, and the phrase was an unnatural one to use without the special force that it would have for him as ἐθνῶν ἀπόστολος. This last phrase, ἐθνῶν ἀπόστολος, about the meaning of which there is no room for doubt, occurs in another of the passages which have a bearing on the present question, xi. 13. After a passage on the rejection of unbelieving Israel, and on God's ultimate purpose involved in it, St Paul turns swiftly round, ὑμῖν δὲ λέγω τοῖς ἔθνεσιν. Here the case is not so clear. As a matter of Greek, I cannot see that there is any difficulty in taking ὑμῖν either as covering the whole Roman Church, in which case no doubt they are as before identified as a body with Gentiles, or as indicating a part of the Roman Church, contradistinguished from a Jewish part, supposed to have been addressed by him just before. The allegation that in this latter case we must have had τοῖς δὲ ἐν ὑμῖν ἔθνεσιν is certainly unfounded. In any case the presence of at least a Gentile element is implied in the words. But though the Greek is ambiguous, the context seems to me to be decisive for taking ὑμῖν as the Church itself, and not as a part of it. In all the long previous exposition bearing on the Jews, occupying nearly two and a half chapters, the Jews are invariably spoken of in the third person. In the half-chapter that follows, the Gentiles are constantly spoken of in the second

person. Exposition has here passed into exhortation
and warning, and the warning is exclusively addressed
to Gentiles: to Christians who had once been Jews
not a word is addressed. Lastly we come to a very
important and difficult passage near the end of the
Epistle, xv. 14—21. We must not pause over its
details, but merely notice that St Paul in *v.* 15, 16
justifies his boldness in writing thus to the Romans by
appealing to the grace which had been given him from
God that he might be a minister of Christ Jesus unto
the Gentiles (εἰς τὰ ἔθνη).

These are the chief passages which point to the
Roman Christians as Gentiles. We must now glance
at one or two passages which have been supposed to
lead to the opposite conclusion. In iv. 1, Abraham
is called 'our forefather [after the flesh]', and it has
been urged that this was true only of Jews. Certainly.
if the passage be taken by itself, this would be the
most obvious interpretation, provided that κατὰ σάρκα
must be taken with τὸν προπατόρα ἡμῶν ; though something might also be said for Weiss's interpretation[1],
that in ἡμῶν St Paul has in view himself and his own
countrymen and not the Romans. But the context
shews that whether εὑρηκέναι is genuine or not, κατὰ
σάρκα belongs not to the preceding words but to τί
οὖν ἐροῦμεν [εὑρηκέναι], being thrown to the end for
emphasis : and if so, Abraham might as well be called
the forefather of both Jews and Gentiles (which is

---

[1] Weiss, *Einleitung in das N. T.* p. 230 n. (ed. 1889).

what the preceding verses suggest) as 'the father of all that believe yet being uncircumcised' (*v.* 11) or 'the father of us all' i.e. both Jews and Gentiles (*v.* 16). This assignation to Gentiles of a Jewish ancestry in the spirit is really less strange than the similar language in which St Paul in writing to the ₁ Cor. x. ₁. Greeks of Corinth calls the whole Jewish people "our fathers" ("all were under the cloud" &c.).

Another passage, to which appeal has often been made, is still more worthy of attention. It is the argument in vii. 1—6 about the limitation of the authority of a law over a man to his lifetime. The phrases which specially are in question are in *vv.* 1 and 4. The argument begins 'Or know ye not, brethren,' γινώσκουσιν γὰρ νόμον λαλῶ κ.τ.λ. Here the supposed reference to Jewish readers rests exclusively on the assumption that νόμος and ὁ νόμος are identical in this Epistle. That is too large a question to argue now : it is enough to say that the supposed identity makes sad havoc of St Paul's sense in many places, though no doubt in the case of this word, as of all Greek substantives, the uses both with and without the article are various, and by no means to be reduced to a single absolute sense. Here it is by no means likely that St Paul has the Jewish law in view, what he says in the immediate context being equally applicable to the Roman law, with which he naturally assumes the Romans to have acquaintance in so simple a matter. But even, if the Jewish Law were meant, all Christians must be presumed to have an amount of knowledge of it sufficient for St Paul's purpose. The evidence of *v.* 4 is quite different and *primâ facie* stronger. " So that, my brethren, ye also were made dead to the law through the body of the Christ, that ye might be joined to another, even to Him that was raised from the dead, that we might bear fruit to God." Here "the law" unquestionably means the Jewish Law, and so there is an apparent implication that the persons addressed had previous to their conversion been bound by the Jewish Law ; and this, it is natural to say, could be true only of Jews. Natural, but not correct. According to St Paul's conception the Jewish Law was God's law for all men, not for Jews only, previous to Christ's coming, just as the Judaizers treated it as binding on all men still. Language closely parallel to what we find here is used by St Paul in writing to the Galatians, who certainly had not previously been Jews. See Gal. iii. 13—iv. 7, where St Paul speaks of himself and the Galatians alike, in words that we might have supposed applicable to Jews only. These passages therefore cannot on examination be held to yield a testimony at variance with that given by the passages in which the Romans are addressed as ἔθνη. The passages which appeal to the Old Testament as a common heritage of course prove nothing. The last thing that St Paul would ever have thought of saying of the Gospel was that it was a new religion. In his eyes, as with all the Apostles, it was the old religion of Israel carried to perfection, not a new faith superseding it ; and so the history and Scriptures of Israel remained the heritage of those who received the new Covenant.

The question however still remains, Is the language which identifies the Romans generally with Gentiles to be taken as exclusive of Jewish Christians? It is hard to think so when we read such chapters as the second and the fourth. Directly addressed to Jewish Christians they certainly are not: but they read as if among the recipients of the Epistle there were men to whom either it was already salutary, or at least it might easily become salutary, to have such words brought before them by way of antidote or prophylactic against ways of thinking which might have too great attraction for them.

A similar inference may be drawn from the remarkable language about the strong and the weak in the fourteenth chapter and the early verses of the fifteenth. Care is needed indeed not to exaggerate the force of the evidence ; and the passage is worth while dwelling upon here for its own sake. Thus much is clear that the Roman Church included persons who had scruples against eating flesh-meat and drinking wine and who observed some special distinction of days (these are called "the weak"); and that on the other hand it included Christians who, like St Paul himself, did not share these scruples (these are called the "strong"); and moreover the whole tone suggests that they either formed the majority of the Church or were at least the most influential part of it. The first party were tempted to judge (κρίνειν, *vv.* 3, 10) the others, accusing them of following a low standard of conscience: the temptation of the second party was to "despise" (ἐξουθενεῖν, *vv.* 3, 10) the others, holding them to be poor superstitious creatures. As regards this moral question of mutual demeanour St Paul holds the balance perfectly even, without in the least concealing with which party he had most personal sympathy. But throughout he does not by a single word hint at the Law, or any kind of tradition, or any kind of authority, or anything affecting the relation of Jew to Gentile, as being concerned in the matter. He treats the matter exclusively from the point of view of individual conscience and faith on the one hand, and love, peace, and mutual building up on the other. Further the nature of the scruples creates a difficulty in referring the division here spoken of simply to a division of Jewish and Gentile Christians. Whatever may be said of the difference of days, abstinence from flesh and from wine was not taught either by the Old Testament or by the ordinary Jewish tradition. Of course abstinence from the flesh and the wine of heathen sacrifices *was* taught: but that cannot be meant here: otherwise we should at least have some hint of the principles laid down in the first Epistle to the Corinthians. The true origin of these abstinences must remain some-

what uncertain: but much the most probable suggestion
is that they came from an Essene element in the Roman
Church, such as afterwards infected the Colossian
Church[1]; and an Essene element implies Judaism,
though not of the strict Pharisaic type. Thus on the
whole this passage suggests that the Roman Church
must have contained at least some Jewish members.

xv. 7—12.

cf. iii. 9,
22—30.

This conclusion is strengthened by the verses which
follow. They begin with words evidently addressed
to both parties alike, inculcating mutual forbearance
and cordiality, προσλαμβάνεσθε ἀλλήλους, appealing to
Christ's similar reception of ἡμᾶς[2], i.e. probably both
Jews and Gentiles: St Paul then goes on λέγω γάρ[3],
thereby making a close connexion with what precedes ;
and the statement so introduced is that Christ became
a minister of circumcision on behalf of God's truth (i.e.
in order to give effect to God's counsels as declared
through the prophets, God's truth being His faithful-
ness in performing what He had spoken); and this
vindication of God's truth St Paul sets forth under
two heads, (1) for the confirming of the promises made
to and concerning the fathers, and (2) for occasion
being given to the Gentiles to give glory to God for

[1] Cf. Col. ii. 16, Μὴ οὖν τις ὑμᾶς κρινέτω ἐν βρώσει καὶ ἐν πόσει ἢ ἐν
μέρει ἑορτῆς ἢ νεομηνίας ἢ σαββάτων.

[2] According to the more probable reading: the other reading ὑμᾶς,
if genuine, would probably refer to the admission of the Gentiles only;
but though well attested (as ἡμᾶς also is) it seems to be a natural
assimilation of person to the imperative προσλαμβάνεσθε.

[3] Not δέ, as the inferior authorities have it.

mercy shown them; and then he adds four quotations from the Psalms and Prophets all of which speak of the nations or Gentiles as joining in acts of faith or praise, and two of which expressly associate Gentiles with Israel ("with His people," "the root of Jesse"). Now if *vv.* 8—12 were detached from what precedes, this significant coupling of Jews and Gentiles, as having each a distinctive share in the blessings brought by Christ, would be sufficiently explained by the general purpose of the Epistle, to which we shall come presently. But seeing that they are connected by that γάρ with *v.* 7, and so with the whole preceding section beginning at xiv. 1, one can hardly doubt that the relations of Jew and Gentile were directly or indirectly involved in the relations of the weak and the strong in the Roman Church. Joint acceptance by the revealed Messiah, accompanied by recognition of diversity, would naturally be set forth by St Paul as a Divine command of *mutual* acceptance in spite of diversity.

On the strength of these indications it is reasonable to conclude that the Church of Rome at this time included Jewish as well as Gentile converts. This is also what might have been anticipated from the historical probabilities or possibilities as to the origin and history of the Church. That is, although it is possible that the first foundation of the Church of Rome was due to Gentile Christians influenced by St Paul's own preaching, this supposition would throw

the foundation to an improbably late date ; and it is
more likely that it took place in the middle period between St Stephen's preaching and St Paul's (so-called)
First Missionary Journey, if not yet earlier in the
first period. In either of these two cases the first
converts would doubtless be chiefly if not wholly
Jews, and this element of the Church would continue
by the side of the later contingent furnished by
heathen converts. As regards the question as to the
numerical proportion of the two elements to each
other, there are no trustworthy data for giving an
answer ; nor is the question of any real importance,
so long as it is taken for granted that both elements
were considerable. St Paul, as we have seen, addresses the Church collectively as of heathen origin ;
but the force of this fact is more positive than negative.
He could not have done so had there been a lack of
Gentile converts, but neither would he, as far as we
can judge, refrain from doing so merely because there
were many Jewish converts likewise : his thoughts
were fixed more on the Church as a whole, occupying
the centre of civilised heathendom, than on such
details as a census would have supplied.

Account must also be taken of the probability
that many of the converts to the Gospel had previously
been converts to Judaism ; that is, in a word, had
been proselytes, whether of the stricter or the laxer
sort. This probable fact will not suffice by itself to
solve the problem of the Epistle to the Romans, as

one eminent critic, Beyschlag[1], has tried to make it do: but it is an important contribution towards understanding the state of things. Obviously the presence of a number of Christians who had belonged both to heathenism and to Judaism would form a connecting link between Christians who had belonged to heathenism alone and Christians who had belonged to Judaism alone, thus hindering the formation of sharp boundary lines and of tendencies towards antagonism. This would especially be the case with those who had belonged to the less strict class of proselytes, and who therefore even before their acceptance of the Gospel had held a position intermediate between Judaism and a devout and purified form of heathenism.

Thus far we have been chiefly considering the question of the previous creed or creeds of the Roman converts. The question of their relation to the great contemporaneous controversy within the Church at large, though not identical with this, is in great measure answered along with it. If the relations between the heathen and the Jewish converts at Rome were such as we have been supposing, it is very unlikely that the Jewish converts were to any great extent Judaizing Christians in the noxious sense of the word. It is an important fact, often overlooked even by great commentators, that Judaizing Christianity as such is hardly at all directly attacked in the Epistle to the Romans, which thus stands in marked

[1] *Theol. Studien und Kritiken*, 1867, p. 627 f.

contrast to the Epistle to the Galatians. Indirectly much that St Paul here says has the gravest bearing on that controversy : but he gives such matter the most impersonal form that he can.

Are we then on the other hand to say that the Church of Rome substantially took St Paul's side against the Judaizers? As far as I see, this would be saying too much. One passage is often cited as at least shewing that the Romans had definitely committed themselves to a distinctive Pauline Christianity, vi. 17, where he says "But thanks be to God, that whereas ye were bondservants of sin, ὑπηκούσατε δὲ ἐκ καρδίας εἰς ὃν παρεδόθητε τύπον διδαχῆς," it being assumed that there is a reference here to a distinctive Pauline τύπος διδαχῆς, contrasted with one or more other τύποι διδαχῆς. Without discussing the details of this difficult and peculiar phrase of nine words, it is enough to say that nothing like this notion of a plurality of Christian τύποι διδαχῆς occurs anywhere else in the New Testament, and further that it is quite out of harmony with all the context. In St Paul τύπος always means either an image of something future or else a personal pattern to be imitated; and so, in accordance with this second sense, the meaning here is "the personal standard of Christian living" (διδαχῆς having rather a moral and religious than a doctrinal force) as opposed to heathen modes of life[1]. Hence

Rom. v. 14.
1 Cor. x. 6.
Phil. iii. 17.
1 Thess. i. 7.
2 Thess. iii. 9.
1 Tim. iv. 12.
Tit. ii. 7.

---

[1] Cf. Eph. iv. 20—24, where ἐμάθετε and ἐδιδάχθητε answer to διδαχῆς here.

the passage has nothing to do with one form of Christianity as distinguished from another. The facts already noticed about Prisca and Aquila leave little doubt that Pauline Christianity had at least some conscious and zealous adherents at Rome, and was not an object of suspicion there: but both the probable historical antecedents and the general tenour of the Epistle suggest rather that the Roman Church presented a favourable soil for the reception of St Paul's Gospel, doubtless combined with personal good-will to himself, than that it was as a body in such a sense definitely Pauline that the teaching of the Epistle would have been in the main a mere recalling to mind of what was already known and believed.

II.

THE PURPOSE OF THE EPISTLE.

A.

EXTERNAL CIRCUMSTANCES.

WE come now, after these preliminaries, to the question what was St Paul's purpose in writing the Epistle. We have considered what can be known or reasonably surmised respecting the state of the Church to which he wrote it, and we may be sure that it was intended to bear very directly on what he knew of the Roman needs at that time. But it is difficult to believe that this single Italian Church alone was in his mind. Various indications suggest that the Epistle was partly prompted by thoughts about the Churches of all lands, and also that it was connected with a peculiar crisis in his own personal life. It will therefore be well to leave Rome for the present, and try to see what light is thrown on the purpose of the Epistle by any particulars in the life and work of the writer, which we must remember were at this time, humanly speaking, the greatest moving power in the enlargement and building up of the Universal Church.

The first great extension of the preaching of the

Gospel beyond the Holy Land to the capital of Syria, Antioch, took place without St Paul. It was due in the first instance to the sporadic teaching of unofficial Acts xi. converts, just as we have seen to have been the case with the foundation of the Church of Rome. The Church at Jerusalem however sent down Barnabas to Antioch and he in turn went to Tarsus and fetched Acts xi. St Paul to Antioch, where they remained and taught. ^{19—21.}

The next step in the spread of the Gospel is what is called St Paul's First Missionary Journey, described in the thirteenth and fourteenth chapters of the Acts. But there is a prelude to this journey which must not be overlooked. We read of Barnabas and Paul being Acts xi. deputed by the disciples at Antioch to carry relief to the brethren at Jerusalem who were suffering from the great famine. By this act the new Syrian Church gave practical acknowledgement of obligations to the original Church of Jerusalem, and St Paul himself was brought afresh into personal friendly relations with the original apostles. After the return to Antioch Barnabas and Paul are sent out by the Church of Antioch in obedience to a prophetic monition, and so the first deliberate official mission begins. The range covered by it is not great. It begins with Cyprus, then proceeds to the neighbouring coastland of Pamphylia on the north-west, and then to the adjoining districts of Pisidia and Lycaonia in the interior. The preaching is accompanied by much resistance and opposition on the part of the Jews. The return is made

3—2

through Pamphylia by sea to Antioch, where the two envoys give an account of their mission.

As the First, so also the Second of St Paul's known Missionary journeys is preceded by a visit to Jeru-

Acts xv. salem. This visit to Jerusalem is a very memorable one. Paul and Barnabas were deputed by the Church of Antioch to confer with the apostles and elders about the question that had arisen owing to the declaration made by certain men coming from Judea that circumcision was indispensable. How grave the crisis was we

Gal. ii.
1—10. can see from St Paul's own account, for there can be no reasonable doubt that the occasion to which he refers is that which is mentioned here by St Luke[1]. Both accounts conspicuously agree as to the cardinal fact that St Peter and St James cordially supported St Paul and recognised his special work. The ratification thus obtained for the Gentile Gospel gave a safe basis for further work among the Gentiles without estrangement from the mother Church of Jerusalem.

Then came what is called St Paul's Second Mis-

Acts xv.
36—xviii.
21. sionary Journey. It begins with labours in confirmation of the results obtained on the former occasion, as well as of the nearer conquests in Syria and Cilicia. Then St Paul penetrates inner Asia Minor, makes his way to the north-west, crosses over to Macedonia in obedience to a vision, thus entering

[1] On this question, and on the difficulties which have quite naturally been felt as to the apparent differences of the two narratives see Lightfoot, *Galatians* pp. 123—128 (ed. 5).

Europe by divine ordinance, not of his own will; goes
to Philippi and Thessalonica, and works his way down
to Athens and Corinth, where he stays one and a half
years. This Missionary Journey is then, in like manner
as the former, followed by a return to Jerusalem, in Acts xviii.
spite of a request from the Ephesian Church that [20—22.]
he would stay there some time. From Palestine he
returns by Antioch and Central Asia Minor till he
reaches Ephesus, where he stays two years. Ephesus Acts xix.
thus becomes his base of operations, as Antioch had [10.]
formerly been.

Now we reach the third set of labours. After
this long and successful stay at Ephesus St Paul sets
out afresh with three objects in view. His immediate
object was the confirmation of the recently founded
Churches of Europe in Macedonia and Achaia. His
ultimate object was a visit to Rome. He did not
however propose, as we might have expected, having
once started westward, to go on further west to
Italy. Between the two westward journeys to Greece
and to Rome he intended to interpose a long east-
ward journey to Jerusalem. The words are worth Acts xix.
notice: "Now after these things were ended Paul [21.]
purposed in the spirit (a curiously emphatic phrase),
when he had passed through Macedonia and Achaia,
to go to Jerusalem, saying, After I have been there,
I must also see Rome." Each of these three purposes
St Paul was, as we know, enabled to carry out, and in
the proposed order: but the details were very different

from what he had evidently anticipated. The story of this journeying fills all the book of the Acts from c. xix. 21 onwards. After a little further delay at Ephesus he reached Macedonia and Greece, where he stayed three months, and during this stay he wrote the Epistle to the Romans. But in order to understand the position of things it is well to recall some leading facts in the events that followed. As St Paul was on the point of sailing direct from Greece to Syria, to go to Jerusalem, he heard of a Jewish plot against him, probably intended to be executed on board ship. He suddenly changed his direction, and went northward round the head of the Aegean. He refused to submit to the delay which would have been involved in visiting Ephesus, but addressed the Ephesian elders at Miletus. He then sailed to Syria, and went up to Jerusalem disregarding the warning prophecies of the brethren at Tyre and of Agabus. Once more he was welcomed by the Church of Jerusalem, and had friendly intercourse with St James, the head of the Christians of the circumcision. At his request he consented to perform a ceremonial act which would shew that he had not in his own person broken loose from the law under which he had been born, in the hope that such an act would have a soothing effect on the minds of uneasy Jewish Christians. Then came the Jewish attack upon him in the temple and his consequent captivity, with its various incidents at Jerusalem and Cæsarea, and finally his voyage as a Roman

prisoner to Rome, which he reaches only after shipwreck and consequent delay.   Thus the three purposes
expressed were all accomplished, though three years
had passed before the final goal, Rome, was attained.
At Rome, as all know, he spent at least two years ;
and from there he wrote what are called the Epistles
of the Captivity.   With subsequent events or subsequent writings we have no special concern in relation
to the Epistle to the Romans.

Now let us consider a little what line of conduct,
what policy as it were, is implied in the leading acts
of St Paul, as interpreted by his own words.   On the
one hand we have the obvious and familiar idea of
him as the Apostle of the Gentiles.   In his own
person he is indefatigable in preaching the Gospel
to the Gentiles, and in paying later visits to stablish
and confirm the Gentile Churches so founded.   He
is also the champion of the Gentile Churches, the
zealous prophet of their calling by God, the defender
of their liberties against the claim set up on behalf
of the Jewish Law as binding on all who would be
recognised as worshippers of the one true God, the
God of Abraham.   This, I say, is obvious.   But
what is no less important, and not so obvious, is his
sleepless anxiety to keep the Gentile and Jewish
Christians in harmony and fellowship with each
other, and himself to act in concert with the original
apostles, never for a moment allowing that they had
any authority over his faith or his actions, but shewing

them every consideration, and doing his best to gain their approval for his own course.

It would have been easy, as it must have been at times most tempting, to sever sharply the hampering links which bound him to the Churches of Judea, and to form the new Gentile Churches into a great separate organisation. But this was just what, he was most anxious to prevent. He could see how great the danger was that such a result might be brought about by the force of circumstances ; and so he set himself with all his might to counteract the tendency. This was doubtless the primary motive— there · may of course have been lesser temporary reasons in each case—which made him visit Jerusalem before each of his great missionary journeys. He would not suffer long absence to cause any coldness to spring up between himself and the authorities of the mother city, as though he had become only a stranger at a distance. Before each fresh outward start he made a point of knitting afresh the old bonds of fellowship and each time anew exhibiting in outward act the principle laid down by Christ Himself, "preaching unto all the nations, beginning at Jerusalem."

Luke xxiv. 47.

One special embodiment and symbol of this reconciling purpose on St Paul's part is the collection on behalf of the Jewish Christians of Palestine, the "saints" as he calls them, which has a considerable place in the Epistles of the second group, those to the Gala-

tians, Corinthians and Romans. We have not time to
go into details of language on this subject. But the
main points are clear, if looked at steadily. Three
main elements can be distinguished in the thoughts
to which St Paul gives expression on this subject.
He was anxious that the various Gentile Churches
should feel sympathy for their Jewish brethren, and
make sacrifices to shew practical Christian fellowship
towards them. He was anxious, secondly, that the
Jewish Christians should accept the offering with
brotherly cordiality and be led by it towards
a warmer and less grudging sympathy with the
Gentile Churches who dispensed with observances
so dear to many of themselves. Thirdly, he was
anxious to be in his own person the living organ
both for the offering of the Gentile gifts and for the
Jewish acceptance of them. For this purpose this
last journey to Jerusalem was absolutely necessary.
Its purpose was the gathering up and crowning of
the purposes of former visits. If only he could
accomplish it successfully, he felt that the most
effectual of all possible steps would have been taken
towards securing the threatened unity of the Jewish
and the Gentile Churches. He would then be able
with full peace of mind to return to the far West
and carry the Gospel across the Mediterranean to the
as yet untouched shores of Spain. On the way he
would be able with full propriety to pay his long
desired visit to Rome itself, the centre of the Empire

Cf. Luke ii. 1.

which embraced Jew and Gentile alike, the place which more than any other by political position represented the universality which he was struggling to secure for the Church. " I know," he wrote, "that in coming to you" (i.e. as the context shews, in coming to you *after* accomplishing this purpose at Jerusalem) " I shall come in the fulness of the blessing of Christ."

Rom. xv. 29.

But this glowing anticipation was blended with anxious misgivings. St Paul had to contend not only with the perversity and narrowmindedness of Jewish Christians, but also with the sanguinary malignity of unbelieving Jews. Just now it seemed as if they were bent on justifying more and more the tremendous language in which he had denounced them long ago. The plot, which, just after this Epistle was written, compelled St Paul to abandon his direct voyage to Syria and take a circuitous route, illustrates the danger which constantly beset him from this source. But in Jerusalem the danger would be greater still: there would be the very focus of hostility, and his enemies could there safely count on a large number of sympathizers among the population. To all this St Paul was not blind, though he resolutely adhered to his purpose of carrying the Gentile offering to the poor brethren of Judea. His keen sense of the danger breaks through various phrases of those seemingly tranquil and almost commonplace verses xv. 22—33. Hitherto,

1 Th. ii. 15 f.

he says, he has been hindered from coming to the
Romans, but " now having no longer place in these
regions," and so on, with language evidently leading
up to a proposal to visit them now : yet he has to
break off ; and says *not* that he is going to *them*,
but that he is going to Jerusalem. Then, later, he
completes the account of what he hoped to do, and
having so said breaks off afresh in an earnest entreaty
to them to join him in an intense energy of prayer,
(wrestling, as it were, συναγωνίσασθαι) that he may
be delivered ἀπὸ τῶν ἀπειθούντων ἐν τῇ Ἰουδαίᾳ,
and that his ministration to Jerusalem may be
acceptable to the saints, that he may come to the
Romans in joy by an act of God's will, and find rest
with them (συναναπαυσώμαι opposed to the συναγωνίσασθαι) ; rest after the personal danger and after the
ecclesiastical crisis of which the personal danger
formed a part. We cannot here mistake the twofold
thoughts of the apostle's mind. He is full of eager
anticipation of visiting Rome with the full blessing
of the accomplishment of that peculiar ministration.
But he is no less full of misgivings as to the probability of escaping with his life. He was utterly free
from the mere passion of martyrdom, which in after
times overmastered many of less apostolic spirit.
His life is full of instances which shew how he held
it to be his duty in ordinary cases to use all lawful
means for escaping from imminent dangers. But he
prepared for this journey with the solemnity of a

sacrifice. It was no mere vague general readiness to suffer death that he professed at Cæsarea when Acts xxi. 13. he rebuked the friends who remonstrated with him for persevering in spite of the warning by the mouth of Agabus, "What do ye, weeping and breaking my heart (or rather enfeebling, distracting it), for I am ready ($\dot{\epsilon}\tau o\iota\mu\omega\varsigma$ $\ddot{\epsilon}\chi\omega$), not merely 'willing,' but already long ago prepared for it, not to be bound only but to die at Jerusalem for the name of the Lord Jesus." This expectation, balanced though it be by the hope that it was part of God's providence for him and his work that he should see Rome, is a measure of the height of importance which he attached to this mission to Jerusalem.

If such was the attitude of his mind towards the future when he was setting out, it was impossible that it should not exercise a powerful influence over the whole writing of an epistle sent forth about this time, and not merely over the few lines in which he directly refers to his own plans. Its words could hardly fail to have something of the character of last words. An interesting confirmation of this is afforded by the only other words of any length of which we have a record as spoken or written by him from this time till his arrival at Jerusalem, namely the address Acts xx. 17—38. to the Ephesian elders at Miletus. Being spoken to the representatives of a Church in the midst of which he had lived and taught so long, it naturally differs much in character from an epistle written to a

Church as yet unseen. But the underlying motive of the whole is the feeling that, according to what he then supposed, the men of Ephesus were destined, as he says, to see his face no more.

The parallelism is not however complete. It is quite possible that by the time St Paul reached Miletus in his journey round the Ægean, his sense of impending danger had become even stronger than it had been a little before he left Corinth: the plot which made him change his course might itself well have that effect, and there may have been other incidents and other tidings unknown to us which would tend in the same direction. But at all events it was impossible that a mere revisiting of Ephesus should stand out before St Paul's mind with the same vivid reality of idea, so to speak, as a first apostolic visit to Rome. Whatever the intervening dangers might be, that imagined arrival at Rome would seem to gain substance from the fitness with which it would crown a Divine order of events. While therefore, as I said just now, the Epistle to the Romans as a whole may be expected to have something of the character of last words, it would not be surprising to find it leaving a space, as it were, for future teaching on other topics, to be built as a superstructure on this foundation. Such an apparent contradiction would in fact be the natural fruit of the contradiction (if one may so call it for want of a better word) in the apostle's own mind, a contradiction due not to any

confusion of mind, but rather to his combination of
the strongest faith in God's providence with the
keenest sense of the mysteriousness of its wisdom,
and the unexpectedness of the ways by which it
often arrives at its ends. It is no paradox to say
that he was too true a prophet of God to be able to
predict his own future.

The length and elaboration of the Epistle may I
think be best explained by the sense, that it might
probably be the writer's last words to the Romans.
If he really expected, as he seems to have done, to be
back in the West and at Rome in a few months, if
only he escaped death at Jerusalem, there was little
apparent need for more than a few lines to explain
his plans, unless he had grave reason to fear that it
might be his last opportunity for speaking to the
Romans in full measure. The sense of the danger
on the other hand, was just what would make him
desirous to ensure the full conveyance of his thoughts
on these matters to Rome, doubtless not without
a prospect that in due course the record of them
would be sent on to other Churches. A final and
orderly review of the subjects discussed would con-
stitute just such a legacy of peace, as it was important to bequeath to all the Churches, if the apostle's
own guiding hand were to be withdrawn by
death.

Much of the Epistle may be called a summing up
of a long and fierce controversy : but it is a summing

up in which the inevitable limitations and antago-
nisms of mere controversy have disappeared. With
the exception of one remarkable passage towards
the end, which we shall have to notice again, Rom. xvi.
there is no reference to opponents throughout. The [17—20.]
matter of controversy is dealt with by way of peaceful
discussion, going down into the fundamental principles
which underlie it. Whether the breadth of treatment
apparent here was but the expression of what had all
along been St Paul's own mental state, or he had
himself risen to serener vision as years went by, we
cannot tell : what is clear is that the serener vision is
here, and that it shews itself near the end of a long
period of conflict. This character of the Epistle,
however independent it may seem of any local circumstances and needs, would, as far as we can tell,
be appropriate to its Roman destination. There was
no need that St Paul should simply fight his old
battles over again for the sake of the Romans if they
were as yet comparatively untroubled by the controversy. On the other hand he could supply them
with no more effectual or less questionable safeguard
against future Judaistic invasion, than this temperate
and orderly and yet most warm and vivid exposition
of principles.

The controversy about law and faith is however
but a part of the great subject of the relation of Jew
to Gentile, and this, quite as much as that controversy,
may be called the subject of the Epistle to the

Romans. Here the doctrinal or universal and the historical or personal elements of the Epistle meet. The carrying of the Gentile offering to Jerusalem to be followed, if successful, by the visit to Rome, is the practical expression of the leading thought of the Epistle, the comprehension of Israel and the nations alike, but in due order, in the final commonwealth of God. And here too there was a correspondence between the purport of the Epistle and its destination. In Rome, the centre of the universal empire, it was easier to realise the new Christian universality than any where else on earth. Nor must we forget that in thus writing to others St Paul was but giving expression to what he felt respecting himself. It must always be remembered that he was himself a Roman citizen, glorying in his Roman citizenship, and sharing Roman ideas. He united indeed all the three principal factors of the civilised humanity of his day, answering to the three languages on the Cross. He was at once Jew, Greek, and Roman; and this personal universality was, if we may venture to say so, essential to his unique office, of at once accomplishing and expounding the true universality of the Church.

The teaching of this Epistle undoubtedly held a very large place in St Paul's total creed, and it relates to what is at bottom, if not on the surface, an issue of deep and vital interest. But it does not follow that this Epistle includes all the important part of St Paul's body of belief. If this were true[1], unless the later Epistles are unreal excrescences we should, as an important school teaches, have to account them spurious. The fact is, St Paul has two comparatively general Epistles, the Epistle to the Romans and the Epistle to the Ephesians, and the contrast between them illustrates both. Both are full of the especially Pauline Gospel that the Gentiles are fellow-heirs, but the one glances chiefly to the past, the other to the future. The unity at which the former Epistle seems to arrive by slow and painful steps, is assumed in the latter as a starting point with a vista of wondrous possibilities beyond. The Epistle to the Romans sketches out how the need of the Gospel arose. It dwells on the failures of the whole ancient world, Jewish and Gentile. In the main it is an exposition of the remedial aspect of the Gospel, that aspect in which it stands in relation to past efforts that had failed.

The Epistle probably further contains the substance of a spiritual autobiography. The Epistle to the Galatians, the most definitely special of all his Epistles to Churches, gives certain outward facts in relation to his apostleship. The second Epistle to the Corinthians unveils the inward conflicts of a peculiar time. But the Epistle to the Romans gives a retrospective experience. St Paul in it interprets

---

[1] From this point the treatment becomes more summary: the MS. is printed as it stands. Edd.

the failure of the old work, Jewish and Gentile, by his own sense of despair as a Jew and as a man. In this Epistle therefore he is not sitting down to teach the Romans what the Christian faith is, still less trying to put one theory of the Christian faith in place of another, a Pauline Christianity in place of somebody else's Christianity, but bringing into clear consciousness for Christians of the metropolis of the world their relation to all their spiritual forefathers, mainly however in the appropriate Roman province— righteousness, belonging to law and morality alike, or the legal aspect of morality, and so Christian duty as part of the new conception and power of right- eousness.

Here we have another limitation and contrast. He is writing to Romans, not Greeks. To Greeks he wrote, partly in the first Epistle to the Corinthians partly in the Epistle to the Ephesians, of Christ as the Wisdom of God in relation to human wisdom and to the knowledge of all truth. But of this in the Epistle to the Romans there is next to nothing ; not because St Paul did not care for it, or had not yet come to care for it, but because he was careful in his stewardship and gave each the fitting portion.

*   *   *   *   *   *   *

APPENDIX ON CHAPTER XVI.

THE structure of the sixteenth chapter is by no
means obvious: and it may be well to say a few
words about it, the more because the differences of
text which occur in the latter part have increased
the confusion, and led to various untenable theories
as to the origin of the different portions of the chapter.
These differences of text concern no mere ordinary
variations, but the presence or absence or transference
of whole verses or passages.

The prayer which forms the end of the fifteenth xv. 33.
chapter, with its solemn ἀμήν, is evidently a special
conclusion to the single glowing sentence, in which St xv. 30—32.
Paul calls upon the Romans to associate themselves
by prayer with his dangerous conflict, that its purposes
may be fulfilled and that he may be allowed to come
in joy and find rest with them. The force of ὁ δὲ
θεὸς τῆς εἰρήνης would then seem to be, "But,
whether I am preserved to come to you thus and so
complete the mission of peace or not, I pray that the
God of peace may be with all of you, so that the

blessing which I am seeking for the Church may at
least descend on you from its heavenly Source."

There is no reason to suppose that the Epistle was
ever meant to end with this prayer. The impassioned
strain of the last few lines was in form a digression
from the external matters of which St Paul had begun
xvi. 1—3. to speak in xv. 22—29. To those matters he now
returns, and completes the unfinished information.
The connexion is, "I have long been wanting to
come to you, I hope to come to you on my way to
Spain if I can bring my Judean mission to a happy
close, but till then I cannot: meanwhile I would
commend to you—i.e. as my representative, so to
speak—Phœbe our sister, who is also a minister of
the Church that is at Cenchreæ." There can be no
moral doubt that Phœbe carried the letter to the
Romans, and her going to Rome may possibly have
given the first impulse to writing. After this com-
xvi. 3—15. mendation we have a long series of salutations to
different persons at Rome, beginning with Prisca and
xvi. 16. Aquila, followed, first by the general bidding ἀσπά-
σασθε ἀλλήλους ἐν φιλήματι ἁγίῳ, and secondly by
a general salutation not from individuals but (strangely
comprehensive language) from "all the Churches of
the Christ." The phrase itself "Churches of the
Christ" is absolutely unique. It occurs only here;
and our familiar phrase "the Church of Christ" (or
"the Christ") in the singular occurs nowhere in the
New Testament: while St Paul speaks several times

of "the Church of God," and twice directly (1 Cor. xi. 16; 2 Thess. i. 4), several times indirectly, of "Churches of God." The nearest approximations to the phrase used here are in Gal. i. 22 ταῖς ἐκκλησίαις τῆς Ἰουδαίας ταῖς ἐν Χριστῷ, and 1 Thess. ii. 14 τῶν ἐκκλησιῶν τοῦ Θεοῦ τῶν οὐσῶν ἐν τῇ Ἰουδαίᾳ ἐν Χριστῷ Ἰησοῦ. In both cases the phrase is used with reference to Judean Churches, which are thus distinguished from unbelieving Jewish ἐκκλησίαι. The unique phrase here used seems meant to mark the way in which the Church of Rome was an object of love and respect to Jewish and Gentile Churches alike, the name Χριστός having its primary significance as it were for the Jew, though this significance was expounded so as to hold good likewise for the believing Gentile: it thus answers to xv. 19 (ὥστε με ἀπὸ Ἰερουσαλὴμ καὶ κύκλῳ μέχρι τοῦ Ἰλλυρικοῦ πεπληρωκέναι τὸ εὐαγγέλιον τοῦ Χριστοῦ) and xv. 29 (οἶδα δὲ ὅτι ἐρχόμενος πρὸς ὑμᾶς ἐν πληρώματι εὐλογίας Χριστοῦ ἐλεύσομαι). Doubtless St Paul had information which enabled him to convey this greeting.

Here St Paul might have ended, merely appending a line of benediction. But before this comes he breaks out in an unexpected direction. Up to this time, as we have seen, he has refrained from direct controversy. Throughout the elaborate expositions and arguments not an antagonist has appeared. Here however at last we have a vehement outburst against certain teachers. It is conceivable that just as St

Paul was on the point of finishing or sending his
letter, fresh tidings reached him of impending doctrinal troubles at Rome.   But it is more likely that
all the time he had been writing the thought was
forcibly present to his mind that the Roman Church
was likely sooner or later to be invaded by the false
teachers, and that he therefore wished to lay a solid
positive foundation which might secure them against
perversion.   It might well be that when he was
reaching the end, with a keen sense that this might
be his last opportunity of saying a word to the
Romans, he became fearful lest the point and bearing
of his expositions should be missed if he gave no hint
of the dangers ahead.   Accordingly he interjects a
warning in emphatic and yet guarded language,
abstaining from any doctrinal catchword, but using
language that would sufficiently interpret itself when
the time came, if it did not now.   The distinguishing
marks of these false teachers are the divisions and the
occasions of stumbling of which they became the
authors, and that, contrary to the teaching which the
xvi. 17, 18. Romans had already received.   They 'serve not our
Lord Christ but their own belly, and they use flattering
and plausible speech' (the precise force of $\epsilon\dot{\upsilon}\lambda o\gamma\acute{\iota}a\varsigma$ is
uncertain, but at all events thus much is contained
in $\chi\rho\eta\sigma\tau o\lambda o\gamma\acute{\iota}a\varsigma$).   There can be little doubt, I think,
that Christian zealots for the Law are meant, not liber-
tine antinomians, as many have gathered from $\tau\hat{\eta}$
$\kappa o\iota\lambda\acute{\iota}a$.   The passage must at all events be taken in

connexion with Phil. iii. 17—21, while that passage
again is illustrated by Col. ii. 20—iii. 4. It is note-
worthy how peculiarly careful St Paul is not to seem
to hint that any of the leaven was already working
in the Romans themselves. His fear only is that
their simplicity and innocence may disable them
from detecting falsehood when they hear it. Their
own obedience (to the Gospel) is, he says, universally
known. He ends this passage with an assurance that
the God of peace, He Whose presence with them he
had implored a few verses above, would indeed not
only be with them but quickly enable them to tread
under foot the adversary, the author of all slander
and all strife.

Then at last comes the benediction " The grace of _{xvi. 20.}
our Lord Jesus [Christ] be with you." The letter is
now complete. It receives however a very natural
postscript. Some of the brethren who were with
St Paul at Corinth, including Timothy, Tertius his
amanuensis, and Gaius his host, express a desire
to add their greetings to the Roman Church. These
greetings end with the words Ἔραστος ὁ οἰκονόμος
τῆς πόλεως, καὶ Κούαρτος ὁ ἀδελφός. Could such
words really stand at the very end of a great and
solemn epistle, even though the actual passage which
they closed were merely a postscript made up of
four short sentences of individual greetings? It is
difficult to think that such an ending would satisfy
St Paul's sense of fitness. And accordingly the best

documents add a very remarkable and pregnant
doxology, τῷ δὲ δυναμένῳ κ.τ.λ. It rises out of
the anxieties just expressed lest the Roman simplicity should be beguiled ("To Him that is able
to stablish you according to my Gospel and the
preaching of Jesus Christ"), and then goes on to speak
of 'the mystery kept silent through the ages but now
at last manifested and proclaimed among the Gentiles,
by means of prophetic scriptures, by command of the
eternal God, the Lord of the ages, unto an obedience
inspired by faith'; and for all this he glorifies "the
only wise God through Jesus Christ unto all ages."
The resemblances of language between this doxology
and later Epistles (especially the Epistle to the Ephesians and the Pastoral Epistles) have often been noticed
and have led, in conjunction with some textual phenomena, to the supposition that it really comes from
a later Epistle, and was subsequently attached to the
Epistle to the Romans. The truth however is that
even in language the affinities of the doxology with
the rest of this Epistle and the Epistles of the same
period are at least as great; while as regards the ideas
of the middle portion of the doxology, their absence
in an explicit form from the early group is explained
by the considerations presented in the second chapter
of the first Epistle to the Corinthians, and by the
immature condition of the Churches at that time. In
substance however these ideas have much in common
with the thought of Rom. viii. 18—30, and still more

with the drift of Rom. ix—xi. They have also the special fitness of restoring to the Epistle at the close its former serene loftiness, after the jarring interruption caused by the necessary interposition of the warning in *vv.* 17—20.

Such is the last chapter of the Epistle as presented in the best MSS. and other authorities, and I believe quite rightly. We have no time for going over all[1] the textual variations, much less discussing them. It is enough to indicate the leading points, neglecting the less important combinations. The benediction which properly comes (20 *b*) after the warning verses, was early (in Western texts) transferred to what seemed a fitter place, after the postscript of greetings. When the verses were numbered in the sixteenth century, it was reckoned as *v.* 24.

The doxology or concluding verses has a more varied history. It was omitted altogether in what is probably the earliest form of the Western text; it was on the contrary duplicated in the Alexandrian text, being inserted at the end of c. xiv. as well as at the end of the Epistle. In the Syrian revision the earlier of the two places was preferred, and in accordance with Western authority it was struck out at the end. The arrangement familiar to us all, by which it stands

---

[1] [See the discussion in the Appendix to "The New Testament in the Original Greek" 1881 ; also the articles in the *Journal of Classical and Sacred Philology*, Vol. ii. iii., reprinted in 'Biblical Essays' by Bishop Lightfoot (1893). Edd.]

at the end of the Epistle and not at the end of c. xiv.,
is one of the most important of the comparatively
few cases in which the Textus Receptus differs from
the Syrian text.   Erasmus here followed the Latin
Vulgate against the Greek evidence accessible to him,
and his collocation of the doxology has been retained
in all the common subsequent editions.   Thus, but for
his retention of the double benediction, in which he had
likewise the support of the Latin Vulgate as known
to him (though not, as it happens, of the best MSS.
of it), the structure of the chapter in the Received
Text would have needed no correction.   There remain critical questions of much interest as to the
cause of the insertion of the doxology after c. xiv. in
the Alexandrian text, the alleged omission of cc. xv.,
xvi. by Marcion, and the undoubted omission of the
doxology altogether in the Western text: but it
would take a disproportionate amount of time to
discuss them now.   There are none of the textual
phenomena which cannot, I believe, be reasonably
explained on the assumption that all the extant
matter not only is by St Paul but belonged to the
Epistle to the Romans as originally dictated by him ;
and that the right order is that to which we are
accustomed in the ordinary editions and in the
English Bible; the only correction needed being the
removal of *v.* 24, that is of the repetition of the
benediction found in its proper place in *v.* 20.

ANALYSIS OF

THE EPISTLE TO THE ROMANS.

I.   i—iv.   Jew and Gentile before God in respect of righteousness.

   i. 1—7.   Salutation, emphasizing the Gospel as a fulfilment, and
the nature of his own Apostleship in relation to the Romans.

   i. 8—17.   Desire for personal fellowship with the Romans, founded
on his debt to all alike, because the Gospel makes known a
Divine righteousness by faith.

   i. 18—fin.   The revelation of a Divine wrath in the moral evil
that followed on refusal to know God.

   ii. 1—16.   Self-righteousness condemned in every quarter.

   ii. 17—iii. 8.   The false and the true privilege of the Jew.

   iii. 9—fin.   No inferiority of the Jew, but all alike, Jew and
Gentile, found wanting, and all alike freely justified by faith
through the redemption in Christ Jesus.

   iv.   The forefather Abraham himself an example of righteousness
by faith.

II. v—viii.   The universal peace springing from the manifested love of God.

   (A summing up of present results with a view to action : but interrupted after v. 11 by a digression on sin, which eventually gives a fuller
sense to these results.)

      v. 1—11.   Plea for peace arising from God's love shewn in
His sacrificing His Son.

v. 12—fin. Christ replaces Adam as the one representative man, bringing life instead of death.

vi. God's grace no incentive to immorality, because the Death is intelligible only as a step to the Resurrection, which involves a new and better life.

vii. 1—viii. 11. The Law becomes at last an instrument of evil, and cannot be the final form of righteousness, which can only be found in the life of the Spirit.

viii. 12—fin. The Spirit or Spirit of Sonship, bearing witness of God's fatherly love, which must be infinite and omnipotent.

III. ix—xi. Jew and Gentile in history according to the counsel of God.

(Comment on the seeming separation of God's own people from God's love [cf. Acts xxviii. 25—28] by reference to His larger counsel. Difficult and uncertain.)

ix. 1—13. The excision of Israelites, and its consistency with retention of Israel.

ix. 14—fin. Justification of God's ways by His supremacy and for manifestation of His full purposes.

x. 1—xi. 12. The Jew's special prerogative of godliness that in which his failure was greatest : reception and rejection of good tidings : the remnant represents the nation : the incoming of the Gentiles the purpose of the Jew's failure.

xi. 13—32. Excision may await the Gentiles : mercy the condition of all reception.

xi. 33—fin. (May be taken with what precedes.) Concluding doxology on the triumph of God's will.

IV. xii—xvi. Fruits of acknowledged mercy. Salutations and last words.

xii. 1, 2. The Christian sacrifice and its probation of God's will (just exemplified in Jew and Gentile).

xii. 3—xiii. fin. Duty within the Christian body, and without the Christian body, both founded on love, shewn forth in works of light.

xiv. 1—xv. 6. The law of love applied to scruples of conscience through mutual bearing of burdens.

INTRODUCTION

TO THE

EPISTLE TO THE EPHESIANS

THE EPISTLE TO THE EPHESIANS.

[*MICHAELMAS TERM*, 1891.]

THE subject on which I propose to lecture this term is the Epistle to the Ephesians. None of the apostolic Epistles more needs the most exact and careful study to ascertain its meaning, and none repays more richly any labour and thought bestowed upon it. A large proportion of its verses is taken up with theology in the strictest and purest sense of the word, the speech of God to man, and especially the meaning of the revelation of God in Jesus Christ. On the other hand the message descending from heaven to earth is preeminently in this Epistle made the foundation of true religion, of the true manner of life in all the great human relations. In the present day the Epistle has a peculiar value, because in various ways its teaching stands in close relation to some of the problems which cannot now but exercise our minds both in theology and in the sphere of practical life. Thus what is true of the Bible generally is specially true of the Epistle to the Ephesians: light falls on the study of it from present experience, and so read, it casts back yet more light for present needs.

But there is no disguising the fact that it is a very difficult book, needing much patience to trace out its meaning, and even then by no means always as yet allowing its precise sense to be discovered. Still no one can work at it with labour and thought without learning much at every step, provided he comes to the book as a learner indeed, not imposing on it the preconceptions which he may have derived from quite other sources. Among those who are proposing to attend these lectures there will no doubt be great differences of capacity and acquirements, and it is obviously impossible to find a style of lecturing which will be equally well suited to all. I am anxious however not to forget the various needs of my hearers, though it may be impossible to avoid what is said seeming at times too elementary for some, and at times too elaborate for others. It is, I believe, well that all divinity students should have some knowledge of the processes which have to be gone through before an apostolic Epistle can be either securely named and its historical place securely determined, or its contents securely interpreted. Nothing more than specimens, as it were, of these and the like processes can by the nature of the case be given within the limits of University lectures: but even from such specimens any attentive hearer, I venture to hope, may gather thoughts and suggestions likely to be of use to him in his own subsequent study of other books of the Bible, in addition to what he may learn respecting the book which forms the immediate subject of the lectures. Much must, however, depend on the amount of personal work which a student puts into the subject before and after hearing lectures upon it. Lectures can never take the place of personal study, and it is not in the least desirable that they should. Their primary office is to stimulate reading and to guide reading; though no doubt they may also be of use in supplying positive instruction in the immediate subject, as regards both facts and the conclusions which may be safely drawn from facts. It is the simple truth that most men have a greatly exaggerated sense of their own incapacity for personal study of such subjects as these. Doubtless there will be always much that has to be taken on trust, whether the authority be a book or a living voice. But there is much also on which every one can exercise his faculties with advantage to himself: and without some preliminary exercise and learning of this kind he is but too likely to listen in a fog, and so to lose whatever chance he might otherwise have of finding interest or instruction.

In dealing with one of the apostolic Epistles, as indeed with many other works of ancient literature,

5—2

three heads of study have to be taken into account, Text, Interpretation, and what is now called Introduction. The determination of the Text means the ascertainment of what the author of the book actually wrote, *i.e.* the detection and removal of blunders or rash changes made by copyists during the period between the writing of the book itself and the writing of the extant manuscripts in which the book has been transmitted to us. On this head I shall say nothing at the outset, merely noticing some of the most important various readings as they may come before us in their turn. One such indeed of peculiar interest we shall have to consider immediately. The Interpretation of the text is the main subject of these lectures. It is not at all probable that we shall be able to get far into the Epistle this term, my purpose being not to set before you a long line of mere opinions of my own as to the meaning of this or that word or sentence : but rather to suggest how their meaning may be worked out with more or less certainty by weighing evidence and tracing connexions of thought. Before however we enter on Interpretation I hope to devote some time to the third head, Introduction, the constituent parts of which will come before us shortly.

This seems to be the best time for saying a little about books. Some of the chief questions belonging to Introduction are still matters of lively debate ; so that no book can be referred to as giving a statement of generally recognised conclusions. In English the

best material coming under this head is to be found in
what are literally "Introductions" to Commentaries.
The older books, which though old are by no means
superannuated, are that of Meyer, the first really great
commentary on St Paul in recent times, well translated, and published by Messrs Clark; and next the
work of our own Alford, which is in a great measure
founded on Meyer, but often shews independent and
usually intelligent judgment, without however special
penetration or originality. A much more recent and
very valuable book is the separate Introduction to
the New Testament by Bernhard Weiss, now made
accessible to English reading in a translation. On
two considerable points belonging to the Introduction
to the Epistle to the Ephesians he seems to me to
take a perverse line, as he does also about some of the
other Epistles. But what he has written is full of good
materials and good observations, well worthy of being
studied. On questions of authorship in particular his
judgments are usually comprehensive and sensible.

Of untranslated German books probably the most
important are Woldemar Schmidt's recasting of the
Introduction to Meyer's Commentaries and Bleek's
Lectures on the Epistles to the Ephesians and Colossians, on the side favourable to St Paul's authorship;
and on the other side, Holtzmann's and Hilgenfeld's
Introductions to the New Testament, the former
following an earlier work of the author devoted
specially to the relations between the Epistle to the

Ephesians and that to the Colossians. The same general line, adverse to St Paul's authorship, is taken in the Introductions to two Commentaries published within the last few months, those of Klöpper and Von Soden.

Of books useful for purposes of interpretation some of the most important names have been already given in the list for Introduction, viz. for English readers the translated Meyer and Alford. To these must of course be added Lightfoot's commentary on the Epistle to the Colossians, as containing much illustrative matter: Bishop Ellicott's editions of both Epistles are likewise useful books of reference on matters of language and grammar. There are no additional German commentaries of exceptional importance, though there are several of considerable value. Woldemar Schmidt, by no means so great a commentator as Meyer, has corrected some of his crotchets, and has the advantage of profiting by the labours of many students down to a much later time; so that on the whole his commentary is the best we have. Others that may be named are Olshausen (now rather of old date, to whom Archbishop Trench was much indebted), Ewald and Harless. Bengel's Gnomon Novi Testamenti, in terse and pregnant Latin, is one of the very few Commentaries that can never become obsolete: twenty-nine only of its pages are required for the Epistle to the Ephesians.

All commentaries are however unprofitable without an assiduous previous use of grammar and lexicon or concordance. Winer's Grammar of the New Testament, as translated and enlarged by Dr Moulton, stands far above every other for this purpose. It does not need many minutes to learn the ready use of the admirable indices, of passages and of subjects : and when the book is consulted in this manner, its extremely useful contents become in most cases readily accessible. Dr Moulton's reference to the notes of the best recent English commentaries are a helpful addition. As regards New Testament Lexicography much remains to be done : but there is abundance of excellent matter in two books of curiously unlike sort, both unfortunately rather dear, Thayer's translation (with enormous additions) of Grimm's general New Testament Lexicon (itself in Latin a cheap and portable book), and Cremer's Biblico-Theological Lexicon of New Testament Greek, now well translated, containing thoughtful but too elaborate and cumbrous articles on select words. Trench's well-known book on the Synonyms of the New Testament, very different in form, has somewhat similar merits and defects, but is much less rich in illustrative passages. More valuable, however, than any lexicon is Bruder's invaluable Greek Concordance to the New Testament. If it be true, as assuredly it is, that the New Testament is best illustrated by itself, *i.e.* by the light which one passage receives from comparison with other passages, a good Greek concordance is the most indispensable of all instruments of study to every Biblical student. Using it patiently and thoughtfully, anyone will soon find the need of the additional help which may be found in commentaries, *i.e.* in the answers which preceding students of the sacred words have found, or thought they found, to the same questions which had suggested themselves to him. But the previous process will have put him in a position to receive real help from the commentaries; and they in turn will in most cases send him back to his New Testament and concordance with subjects for fresh search.

This must suffice about books. We must now enter on questions belonging to Introduction. The most important of these fall under three heads; first, the *Recipients* of the Epistle, secondly, its *Author*, and thirdly, its *Date* and the *Circumstances* under which it was written—and connected with this its *Purpose*. All these points bear closely and directly upon interpretation. The Divine purpose by which the Epistle came to be written and was allowed to become part of our Scriptures of the New Covenant accomplished itself by human means and under human conditions. Just as we are always liable to misunderstand a verse when we detach it from its context of surrounding verses, so also we are liable to misunderstand the drift of the whole Epistle and the meaning of many of its parts when we detach it from its context of historical circumstances; and its context of historical circumstances is but a single phrase combining those various heads of Introduction. Other heads of Introduction concern the history of the Epistle after it was written, its reception in different Churches, or by different writers, and its subsequent preservation in the original and in translations. But these have only an indirect bearing on the greater questions which I mentioned first; and for the most part we shall be able to avoid letting them encroach on our limited time.

For the sake of clearness it is worth noticing at once that those questions of Introduction which cannot be passed over without discussion include in the case of this Epistle some peculiar points which have nothing answering to them in the case of most of the other Epistles. For reasons which will soon appear the question of the recipients is of curious complexity, viz. whether the Epistle was written to the Ephesians only, or to various other Churches only, or to the Ephesians as well as to those other Churches. So also the question of authorship, and thus of purpose, is mixed up with a question as to the relation between this Epistle and the Epistle to the Colossians, and also, though to a less degree, with the question as to the relation between this Epistle and the First Epistle of St Peter.

To prevent the possibility of misunderstanding, it is as well to express at the outset my own firm conviction that the Epistle was written by St Paul. The reasons which have been supposed to enforce a different conclusion will have to be carefully considered presently. But it will be convenient to begin with the less burning question who were the recipients of the Epistle.

I.

RECIPIENTS.

THE title is πρὸς Ἐφεσίους, To the Ephesians. Whatever be the date or authority of that title, of course it does not proceed from St Paul: it expresses simply an early belief or an early tradition, the probable authority of which we must reserve for further consideration. But obviously this title is supported by the common text of *v.* 1, which clearly says τοῖς ἁγίοις τοῖς οὖσιν ἐν Ἐφέσῳ καὶ πιστοῖς ἐν Χριστῷ Ἰησοῦ. This common text, however, is open to the gravest doubts. The greater part of the external evidence unfavourable to it has become known only in quite recent times: yet for some two centuries past a succession of critics have strongly questioned its integrity. The words ἐν Ἐφέσῳ are omitted by the two manuscripts which are not only oldest, but also best, ℵ* B, and by the corrector of a later MS. (67) whose corrections are evidently taken from another quite different MS. of great excellence, now lost. Early in the third century Origen[1], commenting on the Epistle, uses language which shews that these words were absent from his text, *i.e.* his interpretation would be unintelligible if they were present. About one and a half centuries later Jerome[2] shews a knowledge of Origen's interpretation but this cannot count as independent evidence. In the same period, however, Basil[3] refers to the fact that ἐν Ἐφέσῳ was omitted both by predecessors of his (doubtless meaning again Origen) and in the older manuscripts (τοῖς παλαιοῖς τῶν ἀντιγράφων): the way in which he distinguishes these two classes of authorities renders it practically certain that he spoke exactly when he said he had found this reading (ἡμεῖς...εὑρήκαμεν) in those manuscripts.

Going back to Origen's time we find Tertullian reporting a very interesting fact respecting Marcion. We learn from him that Marcion, who is commonly, but not very correctly, reckoned among Gnostics, retained our Epistle in his collections of his favourite apostle St Paul's Epistles, but under

---

[1] (In Cramer's Catena, p. 102). ἐπὶ μόνων Ἐφεσίων εὕρομεν κείμενον τὸ τοῖς ἁγίοις τοῖς οὖσι. καὶ ζητοῦμεν, εἰ μὴ παρέλκει προσκείμενον τὸ τοῖς ἁγίοις τοῖς οὖσι, τί δύναται σημαίνειν· ὅρα οὖν εἰ μὴ ὥσπερ ἐν τῇ Ἐξόδῳ ὄνομά φησιν ἑαυτοῦ ὁ χρηματίζων Μωσεῖ τὸ ὢν οὕτως οἱ μετέχοντες τοῦ ὄντος γίνονται ὄντες, καλούμενοι οἱονεὶ ἐκ τοῦ μὴ εἶναι εἰς τὸ εἶναι, κ.τ.λ.

[2] *Comm. in Ep. ad Eph.* I. 1.   Quidam curiosius quam necesse est putant ex eo quod Moysi dictum sit *Haec dices filiis Israel: Qui est misit me,* etiam eos qui Ephesi sunt sancti et fideles, essentiae vocabulo nuncupatos &c.

[3] I. 255 (*Adv. Eunomium,* II. 19).

the title "To the Laodicenes[1]." This can only
mean (1) that Marcion used the title Πρὸς Λαοδικέας (which we actually find in connexion with his
name in a confused passage of Epiphanius, I. 374 B),
and, (2) that he had no corresponding words in
his text of the Epistle. Had he had ἐν Ἐφέσῳ, the
contradiction would have been too flagrant. Had he
had ἐν Λαοδικίᾳ (a reading of which there is no trace
anywhere), Tertullian, who describes the Epistle as
"according to the verity of the Church intituled 'to
Ephesians'" would assuredly have used strong language
about him, for what he would have assumed to be a
falsifying of the Apostle's own words. It has further
been concluded with great probability that Tertullian's
text likewise did not contain either pair of words,
since otherwise he would have censured Marcion for
omitting them. It is better, however, not to lay much
stress on this inference, as he might possibly be less
impressed by the omission of two words, than by the
change in the whole address of the letter involved in
the change of title.

Thus much at least comes out clearly that the words
ἐν Ἐφέσῳ were absent from at least some manuscripts
early in the second century, early in the third century,

---

[1] *Adv. Marc.* v. 17. Ecclesiae quidem veritate epistolam istam ad
Ephesios habemus emissam non ad Laodicenos : sed Marcion ei titulum
aliquando interpolare (=falsify) gestiit, quasi et in isto diligentissimus
explorator. Nihil autem de titulis interest &c. Cf. c. 11. Praetereo
hic et de alia epistola, quam nos *ad Ephesios* praescriptam habemus,
haeretici vero *ad Laodicenos*.

and late in the fourth century, the geographical regions in the three cases being different; as well as from the three important manuscripts still extant.

How came Marcion, however, to have "the Laodicenes" in the title to his copy of the Epistle? Evidently this fact must somehow be connected with what we read in Col. iv. 16. There St Paul desires that the Epistle to the Colossians after being read in the Colossian Church, may also be read in the Laodicean Church, and, he adds that they themselves, the men of Colossae, should likewise read the letter ἐκ Λαο-δικίας (καὶ τὴν ἐκ Λαοδικίας ἵνα καὶ ὑμεῖς ἀναγνῶτε), which in this context can only mean a letter of St Paul himself received at Laodicea and sent on thence. On the strength partly of this passage, partly of a shrinking from recognition of the former existence of Epistles of St Paul not preserved to us, it has often been supposed not only that the Epistle there spoken of is our Epistle to the Ephesians, but that Laodicea, and not Ephesus, was its real destination, and that Marcion's copy thus bore the only correct title. We must here carefully distinguish the two points, identity with what we call the Epistle to the Ephesians, and exclusive destination for Laodicea. The first supposition is not only possible, but highly probable; but only under conditions which exclude the second. If indeed it were true that our Epistle implies St Paul to be in person unknown to all to whom he wrote it, then no doubt Laodicea would suit better than Ephesus.

But, as we shall see presently, that is not tenable ground ; and in all other respects whatever difficulties there are in an exclusive address to Ephesus, apply in still greater force to the supposition of an exclusive address to Laodicea. It follows that either the Epistle was indeed addressed to Laodicea, but not to Laodicea alone, and that Marcion's copy was derived from the specially Laodicene copy; or that Marcion found πρὸς Ἐφεσίους in the title to his copy, but deliberately changed it to πρὸς Λαοδικέας. If this latter supposition be true, i.e. if he altered the title which he found, then no doubt he did so on grounds of criticism, probably because he thought it must be the Epistle mentioned at the end of Colossians, and so supposed himself to be correcting a nameless title-maker on the authority of the Apostle himself. A phrase of Tertullian seems to imply that this was indeed the case : he would hardly have said " quasi et in isto diligentissimus explorator," if he thought that Marcion was only making an arbitrary guess, rather than performing a critical process. In what sense or senses Laodicea may indeed have had a share in the address of the Epistle we shall see presently. But that has nothing to do with Marcion, if this is the right explanation of Marcion's title. To all appear-ance that title of his attests nothing but the existence of a very ancient text of the Epistle from which the words ἐν Ἐφέσῳ were absent.

Our next step is to consider the textual question,

did these words really belong to St Paul's text or not?
No version omits them, so far as is known. The
evidence of Fathers is ambiguous, because no one not
yet mentioned quotes the verse at all till late in the
fourth century and early in the fifth century, when
we find ἐν Ἐφέσῳ in the Syrian Fathers, and then in
Cyril of Alexandria. But the authorities which do
omit, estimated by what we know of their excellence
elsewhere, afford a strong presumption against the
words.

What then is the Internal Evidence? Here we
come upon those special characteristics of the Epistle
which have long attracted attention. Contrary to
St Paul's custom, one man alone besides himself
is named in it. It was to be carried by Tychicus,
Eph. vi. 21, whom he calls "the beloved brother and faithful
22. minister (διάκονος) in the Lord," whom he was sending
to them to give them tidings of himself, and to
encourage their hearts. St Paul uses as nearly as
possible the same language about Tychicus in writing
Col. iv. 7. to the Colossians. But there the similarity ceases.
In the Epistle to the Colossians we have salutations from several named persons, salutations or
messages to others. It is the same in the little private
Epistle to Philemon, which was evidently sent with
that to the Colossians. Of all this we have nothing in
our Epistle. In both those other Epistles "Timothy
our brother" stands at the head with St Paul himself;
in the Epistle to the Ephesians St Paul stands alone.

This difference in externals that catch the eye is repeated even more remarkably in the inner substance. In the Epistle to the Colossians, and in all St Paul's other writings, the special circumstances, or conduct, or tendencies of the Christians addressed, have left a deep mark on part of the Epistle, or on the whole of it. But nothing thus special and limited can be recognised in the Epistle to the Ephesians, the little that is said of its destined recipients being couched in quite general language. In the Epistle to the Colossians much of the teaching is manifestly controversial, directed against mischievous tendencies at work in the Church addressed. In the Epistle to the Ephesians there are no clear or express warnings of this kind: from first to last the teaching, whether theological or religious, is exclusively positive in form; whatever reference there may be to tendencies dreaded is exclusively indirect. These are characteristics which would most naturally be found in a letter addressed to a number of Churches, differing from each other in circumstances, condition, and personal relations with the writer of the Epistle. It would be difficult on the other hand to account for them in an Epistle addressed solely to the Church of a single city, above all, if that city were Ephesus.

Let us pause here a little to consider what the

past relations between this Ephesian Church and St
Paul had really been. The evidence all lies on the
surface of the New Testament, but its full significance
does not always make itself felt without a little
consideration. In St Paul's first 'missionary journey,'
as everyone will remember, he entered what we call
Asia Minor from the south, and penetrated northward
inland, without swerving westward to the great cities
on or near the Ægean. On his second journey, after
visiting and stablishing the Churches founded on that
former occasion, he was apparently making his way
to Proconsular Asia, doubtless specially meaning to
preach in its great capital Ephesus, when he received
a Divine warning which led him to pass onwards
further to the north-west: St Luke's words are "being
Acts xvi.6. hindered (plural, i.e. Paul and Timothy and Silas)
by the Holy Spirit from preaching the word in Asia."
Other monitions led him on across the Hellespont,
and so he found himself carrying out a succession of
European missions, while Ephesus, the chief city of
Asia Minor, still lay behind him untouched. On his
return to the East, though he had little time to spare,
it would seem that he could not be satisfied without
at least setting foot in Ephesus, and making some
small beginning of preaching in person there. He
left Aquila and Priscilla to carry on the work:
Acts xviii. but he himself entered into the synagogue according
19. to his usual practice, and reasoned with the Jews.
Then resisting all entreaties to remain, he said fare-

well with a promise to return again if God should will, sailed to Palestine, visited first Jerusalem and then Antioch, where he stayed some time, and then followed his old course through southern Asia Minor, and this time was allowed to follow it right on to its natural goal, Ephesus. How closely in St Luke's view that first short visit to Ephesus was connected with this second much longer visit, may be inferred from the extraordinary brevity with which he gathers together the three long journeys to and from Ephesus, dispatching them in five or six lines. The whole story gains in point and clearness if we suppose that it is essentially a record of the steps by which St Paul was enabled to carry out a cherished desire, to be himself the founder of a Christian Church in that great metropolis in which the East looked out upon the West. His desire was granted, and moreover Ephesus was the only city of the first rank which, so far as any trustworthy evidence goes, had as its founder either St Paul or any other apostle.

As a prelude to St Paul's arrival at Ephesus this second time, we are told of Apollos' reception and instruction by Aquila and Priscilla. Then comes the incident of the men who had received only the baptism of John the Baptist, St Paul's preaching in the synagogue for three months, and then, when this course was hindered by the resistance of unbelieving Jews, his forming the disciples into a separate body in Tyrannus's lecture-hall. Next comes a compre-

Acts xviii. 18—23.

hensive verse, "and this continued for the space
of two years, so that all they which dwelt in Asia
heard the word of the Lord, both Jews and Greeks,"
followed by an account of St Paul's miracles, and of
the incident which led to the burning of the magical
books. Of this long period (two years and more),
during which St Paul was building up the Ephesian
Church we know little. It does not seem to have
been quite without interruptions, but probably these
interruptions were few and brief[1]. On the other hand,
as is proved by allusions in the Epistles, it must have
been a time of sore anxieties to St Paul about the
state of other Churches, and of dangers and sufferings
encountered by him in his own person[2]. But at this
stage in the course of events, we are led by the Acts
to regard Ephesus as the centre and starting point of
Gentile Christendom, just as the Syrian Antioch had
been at first, when the Gospel had gone forth beyond
Jerusalem and Judea, and as Rome was to be presently, from the time marked by the end of St Luke's
narrative.

When at last St Paul had decided to leave
Ephesus for a series of long journeys ending at Rome,
the great tumult occurred which was stirred up by
Demetrius in the name of Diana of Ephesus. After
this memorable occurrence St Paul set forth on his
journey into Macedonia and Greece. Then returning

---

[1] See Lightfoot, *Col.* 30 f.
[2] Lightfoot, *Gal.* 38 ff.

from the west, and making his way to Jerusalem, once more he craved converse with Ephesus, though too much pressed for time to risk the delay which a visit there might bring; and so from Miletus he sent for the elders of the Ephesian Church, and gave them those peculiarly solemn warnings, in which he reminded them of his own labours among them, and told them that they would see his face no more.

Let us now gather up in our minds these successive stages in the relations between St Paul and the Ephesians—his original desire to preach among them, checked for the time by a Divine warning, his reception on his first short visit when he left his two trusty associates behind, the two or three long and evidently eventful years during which Ephesus was his home, and lastly the summons to the rulers and teachers of its Christian community to meet him and receive what he then believed to be his last admonitions. Having so done, if we turn to the Epistle and read it through, we cannot but marvel how it could be so entirely devoid of all traces of such rich and heartfelt experiences, if it really was addressed to the Ephesians alone. No doubt the difficulty does not exist for those who say that the Epistle was not written by St Paul at all, but by some one in his name, to whom the Ephesian Christians suggested themselves as persons to whom St Paul might naturally be supposed to write. But, apart from the improbability that an epistle should be thus fictitiously written without the slightest attempt to infuse any local ҫolour, we shall presently find ample reason for accepting its genuineness. If however it is genuine, these characteristics which we have been considering suggest that, if addressed to the Ephesian Church, it must have been likewise addressed to other Churches, whose circumstances in relation to St Paul were entirely different. This inference is quite independent of the external or documentary evidence for omitting ἐν 'Εφέσῳ : but evidently they afford strong support to each other.

Before we go on to consider what kind of destination for our Epistle would be at once most probable in itself and most in accordance with these conditions, we had better finish what is involved in the question whether on the whole internal evidence does or does not sustain the omission of ἐν 'Εφέσῳ. It is alleged that the omission of these words leaves a sentence which yields no reasonable meaning. Certainly no one could now be satisfied to follow Origen and Basil in putting a transcendental force into τοῖς οὖσιν—"the Saints that ARE," as partaking of Him Whose name is I AM. But, as meaning "the saints who are also faithful in Christ Jesus," the phrase would be by no means the unmeaning platitude that it is sometimes said to be ; since it might indicate the combination of

the old title of 'saints' belonging to ancient Israel with
the distinctive characteristic of Christians. On the
other hand this way of referring indirectly to those who
once had been called 'saints,' ill suits the tone of the
Epistle, especially as those addressed are treated as
having been heathens. And it is a still more serious
objection, that both words stand together in no such
antithetical sense in the opening salutation of the
Epistle to the Colossians τοῖς ἐν Κολοσσαῖς ἁγίοις καὶ
πιστοῖς ἀδελφοῖς ἐν Χριστῷ. Though however the
simple omission of ἐν Ἐφέσῳ would undeniably leave
an awkward and improbable phrase, the same cannot
be said if the omission is replaced either by alternative names preceded by ἐν, or by a blank space
such as might be somehow filled up in this manner.
Supposing a plurality of Churches to be intended to
be recipients of the Epistle, such a plurality of alternative geographical names or such a blank would be
natural enough.

The suspicion that others besides the Ephesians
were intended to be the recipients of the Epistle, goes
back as far as Beza, the great Genevan commentator
of the latter part of the sixteenth century, who in a
note on the subscription at the end says "Sed suspicor
non tam ad Ephesios ipsos proprie missam epistolam,
quam Ephesum ut ad ceteras Asiaticas ecclesias
transmitteretur[1]," which, he adds, perhaps induced
some to omit ἐν Ἐφέσῳ. The same view is worked

[1] p. 288 (ed. 1598).

out more fully by Archbishop Ussher in his Annales
Veteris et Novi Testamenti[1]. Referring to the evidence of Basil and Jerome, he translates the Greek
without ἐν 'Εφέσῳ thus "vel ut in literarum ency-
clicarum descriptione fieri solebat sanctis qui sunt
* * * * et fidelibus in Christo Jesu"; as if, he proceeds, it had been first sent to Ephesus, as the chief
metropolis of Asia, to be thence transmitted to the
remaining Churches of the same province, with the
name of each inserted: and as if some of them,
whom Paul himself had never seen, were chiefly
referred to in those words of his (he quotes i. 15;
iii. 2), which Marcion perhaps regarded as suiting the
Laodicenes, who had not seen the apostle in bodily
presence, rather than the Ephesians with whom he
had so long held converse.

This suggestion of Ussher's, that the letter was
what the Greeks called an encyclical letter, a letter
sent on a round of successive places and that the
omission of ἐν 'Εφέσῳ should accordingly be interpreted as a gap left blank, supplies the essential
points for an explanation which really suits the facts,
though Ussher fails to notice the confirmation which
it receives from the contents of the letter. That an
Epistle should be practically encyclical is not unex-
ampled in the New Testament. The First Epistle of
St Peter was to be carried round by Silvanus, in his
journey through most of what we call Asia Minor, the

1 Pet. i. 1,
v. 12.

---

[1] *Aetas Mundi*, vii. p. 680 (ed. 1673).

provinces in this case being named. How the Apocalypse was to be conveyed, we do not know : but in its
epistolary aspect it in a manner combines encyclical
and so to speak individual characteristics. It includes
an epistle addressed to each of seven representative
Churches of Proconsular Asia; while the whole book
was addressed to them all.

But we have still to consider the questions, (1) as
to its identity with the Epistle called by St Paul "the
Epistle from Laodicea," and (2) as to the inclusion of
Ephesus itself in the circle of places to which it was to
be carried. We have already seen that if our Epistle
is identical with the "Epistle from Laodicea," then it
cannot have been definitely addressed to the single Laodicean Church as our Epistle to the Colossians was to
the Colossian Church: its internal character makes that
incredible. Either then the "Epistle from Laodicea"
was indeed addressed singly to Laodicea, but is a lost
letter entirely unknown to us ; or it was our Epistle to
the Ephesians, having neither more nor less to do
with Laodicea than with other cities of that region,
and the notice of it under a name connected with
Laodicea must be due only to local causes.

The former supposition is not incredible, but St
Paul's language contains indications which make it
highly improbable. First writing to Colossae, he sends
greetings to the brethren in Laodicea. This would Col. iv. 15.
be a strangely circuitous proceeding if he were at
the same time writing a letter of the same kind to

Laodicea; but it is quite intelligible if Laodicea was to receive only an encyclical letter, by its very nature unfitted to contain personal greetings. Again, though the phrase τὴν ἐκ Λαοδικίας can be justified by classical precedents as an ordinary case of attraction, it cannot be said that such figures of speech are in St Paul's manner. It is more probable that he purposely avoided saying τὴν εἰς Λαοδικίαν just because it would suggest a letter written specially to Laodicea, whereas the use of ἐκ would have merely a formal, not a practical ambiguity, and this would rather suggest a letter carried on (or forwarded on) from Laodicea, as an encyclical letter would be.

This supposition, therefore, of an encyclical Epistle, of which Laodicea was one of the recipients, remains finally as alone satisfying the conditions. Two points have to be noticed here; (1) personal, as to its mode of conveyance; (2) geographical, as to the position of Laodicea and Colossae. It was conveyed, we can see, by Tychicus, who probably went on a series or tour of visits to different Churches.

About the course and limits of his journey we know nothing. The usual supposition is however probably correct that the Churches which Tychicus visited were those of Proconsular Asia, the region most nearly associated with St Paul's long stay at Ephesus. Proconsular Asia was also Tychicus's own native province, as we learn from Acts xx. 4, Ἀσιανοὶ δὲ Τυχικὸς καὶ Τρόφιμος. Indeed, since

Trophimus, here coupled with him, was an Ephesian, it is often inferred that Tychicus was an Ephesian too. But St Luke's words, carefully read, rather suggest that he was not an Ephesian. They stand at the end of a list of seven companions of St Paul in his last journey from Greece to Jerusalem, and four out of the preceding five have their city mentioned, not their province; one is from Beroea, two from Thessalonica, one from Derbe; Timothy (about whom enough had been said in a former chapter) being the fifth. We should therefore have expected Ἐφέσιοι here, had both Tychicus and Trophimus been from Ephesus; and the substitution of Ἀσιανοί suggests that St Luke was glad to speak of their common province because they had not a common city. To what part of Proconsular Asia Tychicus belonged we cannot in the least tell: but the language of Col. iv. 7—9, especially the contrast with the Colossian Onesimus, suggests that he did not come from the district to which Colossae belonged.

It can hardly be necessary to remind any one who has read ever so little of Lightfoot's Commentary on the Epistle to the Colossians, how vivid a picture is there[1] drawn of this district, the region in which "the Churches of the Lycus" were planted. He describes the great city of Hierapolis and the still greater city of Laodicea, facing each other some

[1] *Epistle to the Colossians*, pp. 1—22.

distance apart on each side of the Lycus, one of the rivers tributary to the Maeander, and then, some ten or twelve miles higher up, the much smaller city of Colossae on the very banks of the river. He reminds us (pp. 17 ff.) that though in one sense belonging to Phrygia this district belonged politically in St Paul's time to the provinces of Asia, of which it formed a remote and distinct part. We have an indication of the close connexion between these three young Col. iv. 13. Christian communities in St Paul's words about Epaphras the Colossian, how he had much toil for the Colossians and for them in Laodicea and for them in Hierapolis. But evidently there were special perils threatening the Church at Colossae which called forth a special letter to them, perils not improbably arising out of proximity to Phrygia proper, though it would also be well that the Laodicenes should hear what it contained.

Whether the blank in the text of the encyclical epistle was only a blank, or whether for each city it was filled up with the local name, is wholly unimportant. It is possible but hardly likely that St Paul would provide Tychicus with a number of copies, one for each Church. It seems more natural that Tychicus should carry with him the one original Epistle with a blank space, that in each Church the local name should be orally inserted when the letter was publicly read aloud on Tychicus's arrival; and perhaps that if, as we should expect, a copy were taken

for local preservation before Tychicus passed on to
the next city, the local name should be inserted in
writing in such local copy. The only gain, however,
of such speculations is to give reality and shape to
our conception of the Epistle, not as constituting a few
pages of our Bible, but as an actual letter carried
actually round and read to gatherings of eager
listeners for whom it was expressly written.

But to return to weightier matters, if our Epistle
was an encyclical letter, the question still remains
whether it has any right to bear its present title.
Was Ephesus itself part of the circle? If it was the
chief cities of Proconsular Asia that formed the circle,
it would a priori be natural to expect the circle to
include the capital. Here, however, we are met by
certain passages which undeniably at first sight
suggest that the persons to whom they were written
had had no personal intercourse with St Paul, much
less such long and close intercourse as we know the
Ephesian Christians to have had with him.

The least important is the first, "Wherefore I Eph. i. 15.
also, hearing of the faith in the Lord Jesus that is
in yourselves and that ye shew toward all the Saints."
This is language not likely to have been chosen
without some accessory words if a Church founded by
the Apostle were alone addressed. Accordingly
Theodore of Mopsuestia, the most acute of ancient
critics who have left commentaries on St Paul, assumes
on the strength of these words that the Epistle must

have been written before St Paul visited Ephesus[1]; and he is followed by other Greek writers (see Dr Swete's note). But, while in the strictest sense appropriate to the great mass of the Churches just addressed, Churches with which St Paul had no personal acquaintance, it would not be inappropriate in reference to tidings about the *present* condition of the Ephesian Church, from whom, according to the most probable date of the Epistle, he had now been separated for a considerable time. It is likewise worth notice that, while very similar language is used to the Colossians, in their case St Paul says expressly some way further on "I would have you know how great a striving I have for you and for them at Laodicea and *for as many as have not seen my face* in the flesh." We must reasonably have *a fortiori* expected some such words as these last to occur somewhere in our Epistle, if it was addressed exclusively to Churches who had had no personal contact with the Apostle.

The other two passages are of a different kind, though they in like manner turn on the word ἀκούω which is applied however to "hearing" on the part of the recipients, not of the writer. They resemble each other still more closely, as both containing the phrase εἴγε ἠκούσατε, "If so be that ye heard (or 'have heard')." In the first of them we read "For this cause I Paul, the prisoner of Christ Jesus, on behalf of you Gentiles,

Col. i. 4.

Col. ii. 1.

Eph. iii. 2.

---

[1] Professor Swete: *Theodore of Mopsuestia on the Minor Epistles of St Paul* (1880), vol. I. p. 112.

—if so be that ye have heard of the stewardship of that grace of God which was given me to you-ward," explained further on as meaning "that the Gentiles are fellow-heirs." How was it possible, it is asked, that St Paul should have a shadow of doubt whether the Ephesians, of all men, had heard of that Divine stewardship of his, his special mission to the Gentiles? Must he not have been exclusively addressing Churches with which he had come into no contact? The usual answer to these questions is, I think, a true and sufficient one. The compound particle εἴγε, though it never can mean 'since' but remains always an intensified "if," is not unfrequently used with a rhetorical or appealing force where no real doubt is meant to be expressed[1]. This appealing force is fully expressed here by the context. St Paul is going to plead the cause of Christian holiness as against Gentile indulgence towards vice as one entitled to speak as a prisoner who owed his imprisonment to his zeal for the true welfare of Gentiles: but having made this claim, before he catches up and completes his pleading, he turns aside to ask, as it were, in these iv. 1, 17. words whether they were not pledged to accept the validity of that claim by their knowledge of the special charge divinely entrusted to him. But this is not all. If it is incredible that St Paul should have had real doubts whether the Ephesian Church had heard of that special charge, it is only a shade less

[1] See Bishop Ellicott's note.

incredible that any Church of Proconsular Asia should have remained in similar ignorance. The Colossian Christians, in one of the remotest corners of the province, had, we know with moral certainty, received their faith not from him but from his disciple Epaphras[1]; and there can be no reasonable doubt that it was by men like Epaphras that the Gospel was carried through the province during St Paul's long stay at Ephesus, when "all that dwelt in Asia heard the word of the Lord, both Jews and Greeks." Thus the appealing force of εἴγε, as distinguished from its doubting force, is alone possible here if the writer was St Paul.

Col. i. 7.

Acts xix. 10.

In the remaining passage St Paul again uses εἴγε with an appealing force, though not now on his own behalf but on behalf of his readers. "But ye did not so learn the Christ; if so be that ye heard him, and were taught in him, as truth is in Jesus; that ye put away, as concerning your former manner of life, the old man &c." That is, he appeals to that historical Gospel of Jesus of Nazareth which they had originally received as fixing the moral standard of the highest Christian faith. On the other hand it is inconceivable that about any Church of Proconsular Asia, any more than about the Ephesian Church, St Paul could have expressed a real doubt whether they had heard Christ, at least in any sense compatible with the context. Thus both these passages, if they

Eph. iv. 21.

---

[1] See Lightfoot, *Colossians*, pp. 24—31.

prove anything about the Churches addressed, prove too much : that is, they have no real bearing on the question whether the Ephesian Church was among these Churches.

Accordingly we are brought back once more to the traditional title πρὸς ’Εφεσίους. Of its precise date or origin we know nothing. But we do find the Epistle cited under this name by the five chief fathers of the three-quarters of a century ending in the middle of the third century, the period when first with the rarest exceptions the titles of books appear, viz. Irenaeus, Clement of Alexandria, Origen, Tertullian, Cyprian ; and nowhere do we find a trace that any other title existed except in Marcion's case, and he, as we saw, probably represents not a tradition but a criticism. Even a title thus carried back to the second century, and probably to an early part of it, would have no decisive authority against really strong evidence of other kinds. But it must carry considerable weight if in the text itself ἐν ’Εφέσῳ is entirely spurious, and not less if these words have been truly transmitted from one original of the Epistle, though not from others. It would also be difficult to think of St Paul as excluding Ephesus from view in writing to a circle of Churches of Proconsular Asia an Epistle having the character and purpose which we shall, I hope, presently find to belong to our Epistle. Thus, on a review of the whole evidence, we are led to the conclusion that the familiar title may rightly be

H. R.   7

considered defective or inadequate in so far as it gives
no indication of the varied range of Churches to which
the Epistle was sent; but that so far as it goes it is true.
If we have an adequate sense of what Ephesus was to
St Paul, we cannot but feel' that there is a true and
worthy fitness in the association of our Epistle with
the Ephesian name.

II.

TIME AND PLACE OF WRITING.

WE have now considered all the most essential points respecting the destination of our Epistle, the question, that is, who it was that St Paul had in mind when he was writing. The next great question, whether St Paul himself was indeed the writer, may with advantage stand over a little to be considered with some cognate questions as to the purpose of the Epistle. It will be most convenient to take now a more external question, in this respect resembling that which we have hitherto been considering; to ask at what time and place the Epistle was written, on the assumption that St Paul wrote it. For this purpose we are able to use the evidence supplied by the Epistles to the Colossians and to Philemon, as they were evidently carried by Tychicus on the same journey.

The most obvious mark of external circumstances is the language about imprisonment, "I Paul the Eph. iii. 1. prisoner of Christ Jesus"; "I therefore the prisoner iv. 1.

Col. iv. 3. in the Lord"; "to speak the mysteries of the Christ,
i. 24.   for which I am also in bonds (δέδεμαι)" (cp. "now I
iv. 18.   rejoice in my *sufferings* for your sake"); "Remember
Philem. 1 my bonds"; "Paul a prisoner of Christ Jesus"; "Paul
9.   an ambassador and now a prisoner also of Jesus
10.   Christ"; "my child, whom I have begotten in the
13.   bonds, Onesimus"; "that in thy behalf he might
minister to me in the bonds of the Gospel."

What imprisonment then is meant? There are only
two which are worth considering, each of them two
years long, both closely connected historically and
separated from each other by only a few months; yet
differing remarkably from each other in the associations
which they respectively suggest. They are of course
the imprisonment at Caesarea, and the imprisonment
at Rome. St Paul had come for the last time to
Jerusalem to bring the Gentile offering, where he
was rescued from a murderous plot of the Jews by
the chief captain Lysias, who sent him by night
with a guard of 200 soldiers to Caesarea. There
he was in charge of Felix the Roman Proconsul,
Caesarea being the civil capital of Palestine since
the time of Herod the Great, who built it, a mag-
nificent seaport town between Joppa and Mount
Carmel. Two years later, Felix was succeeded by
Festus, and after a hearing by him in company
with Agrippa, St Paul was sent forth on his Rome-
ward journey, which was interrupted for the winter
by the shipwreck. The last sentence of the Acts

leaves him still a prisoner at Rome after two years more.

Now it used to be assumed without question that the three Epistles, to the Ephesians, to the Colossians and to Philemon were written in the Roman captivity. On the other hand for the last half century or thereabouts a considerable body of critics, including some distinguished for sobriety of judgment, have referred them to the Caesarean captivity. Such evidence as we have seems to me to go the other way, and to support the old view. But the whole evidence of what may be called a historical or a literary kind is curiously scanty in amount, and probably few who have not had occasion to look into it would imagine how rash it would be to express a confident opinion without close examination. As we shall see presently, the decision is by no means a matter of idle curiosity, but intimately connected with interpretation.

The first piece of evidence is connected with the Epistle to the Philippians. That Epistle, you will remember, is no less a Captivity Epistle than the three which we have now in hand. Four verses of the first chapter contain references to the Apostle's (present) Phil. i. 7, bonds; there is no other clear link connecting the 13, 14, 17. one Epistle with the three. Still it is but right to ask whether it was written before them or after them. Now it is very widely believed that it was written very late in St Paul's captivity at Rome and after our three. Very few refer it to the Caesarean time. This part of the subject has been so admirably worked out by Lightfoot in the essay headed "Order of the Epistles of the Captivity" in his commentary on this Epistle[1], that I will not take up time with going over the ground now. Lightfoot urges with great force, that there is no real weight in the arguments, chiefly four, which are commonly put forward as decisive for a very late date for the Epistle to the Philippians, the most plausible perhaps being a comparison of the persons named as present with St Paul in the several Epistles. Against these at best inconclusive considerations he urges the less catching but more substantial evidence of style and language. This, he shews, is intermediate between the style and language of the earlier Epistles and those of our triad : in particular the affinities with the Epistle to the Romans, the last of the earlier Epistles, are very great. If this is the right conclusion, as I fully believe it to be, our three must of course have been written in the Roman captivity, since their predecessor was likewise.

It would not be right however to leave the matter here, Lightfoot's view about the position of the Epistle to the Philippians having so few friends. We must therefore go on to consider how the evidence lies when that Epistle is excluded from view. Here we shall have little help from Lightfoot except on one important historical point on which his remarks are of special

---

[1] *Epistle to the Philippians*, pp. 30—46 (ed. 1878).

value. We should have had more from his pen on the subject had his proposed edition of the Epistle to the Ephesians ever been written.

We may begin with a few words from Weiss, the most competent of the champions of Caesarea. Discussing the question whether the Epistles to the Colossians and to Philemon were written at Caesarea or at Rome, he writes[1], "Much that is untenable has been "urged for the one as for the other view. But what "is quite decisive is the fact that according to Philip- "pians ii. 24 Paul intended to proceed from Rome to " Macedonia in the event of his being set free, whereas, "when he wrote Philemon 22 it was his wish to go "immediately to Phrygia; and the manner in which "he already bespeaks for himself lodging in Colossae "for his visit there makes it altogether unlikely that "the letter was written in Rome, where moreover in "the course of a regular judicial proceeding Paul could "never reckon so definitely on his liberation."

Three points are involved here. First, the difference of destination on being set free. Here there are two obvious answers. Between writing the two Epistles, St Paul might well have found reason to change his mind as to his course on his release: first, Macedonia and Philippi might seem to claim him most, and then Asia and Colossae, or vice versa. And again even this supposition is not necessary, for he might well take Philippi on his way

[1] Weiss, *Einleitung in das Neue Testament* (Berlin, 1889) § 24, c. 2.

from Rome to Colossae, Philippi being, as Lightfoot says[1], on the great high road between Europe and Asia, so that Ignatius passed it when he was brought from Asia to Rome.

Philemon 22.

The next point urged by Weiss is the greater nearness of Colossae to Caesarea than to Rome with reference to the request to prepare a lodging. But in truth both places are far too distant from Colossae to make the request intelligible in its crude literal sense. How little St Paul meant Philemon to take it thus is tolerably clear from his next words, "for I hope that through your prayers I shall be granted to you"; not granted to you soon, but simply granted to you, and of this there is no more than a hope. Had St Paul been really expecting a speedy release, we may be sure there would have been some trace of it in the Epistle to the Colossians. What seems to be the true sense here, or something like it, is hinted by Jerome[2]. St Paul spoke to Philemon not in strict truth (*vere*) but *dispensatorie* (doubtless οἰκονομικῶς) *ut dum eum exspectat Philemon ad se esse venturum, magis faciat quod rogatus est.* It is but a playful way of saying to Philemon, "Remember that I mean to "come and see with my own eyes whether you have "really treated your Christian slave as I have been "exhorting you"; and then giving the thought a serious turn by assuring him that, 'coming is no

---

[1] *Philippians*, p. 48 f.
[2] *Comment. in Ep. ad Philemonem*, v. 22.

mere jest, for he does indeed hope some day to
be set free through their prayers, and then he will
haste to visit them.'

As regards the third point the comparative possibilities of looking for a speedy release, at Rome and at
Caesarea, we really have very little material for judg-
ing. But thus much is plain that, when the prosaic
interpretation of the bespoken lodging falls away,
the language to Philemon with reference to future
release is even more wanting in definite anticipation
than the language to the Philippians.

More really plausible than these three arguments which Weiss thinks decisive for Caesarea
is the comparison of dates with reference to earthquakes which visited the cities of the Lycus about
this time. This is the matter which I referred to
as illustrated by Lightfoot[1], who has carefully con-
structed a list of the earthquakes known to have
devastated that region in various ages. The only
points however which concern us here are these.
Under the year 60, the year which includes the last
part of St Paul's Caesarean imprisonment, Tacitus
states that "Laodicea, having fallen down (prolapsa)
by an earthquake, recovered itself by its own re-
sources without help from us (i.e. from public
funds)[2]." Four years later, at the time of Nero's setting
Rome on fire, Eusebius's Chronicle states that "three

[1] *Epistle to the Colossians*, pp. 37—40, ed. 1875.
[2] *Ann.* xiv. 27.

cities in Asia, Laodicea, Hierapolis and Colossae, fell down (conciderunt) by an earthquake[1]." On the double assumption that these two statements refer to the same event and that Tacitus is more to be trusted for the year than Eusebius, it is urged that an Epistle addressed by St Paul to Colossae, if written from Rome, would naturally have contained some allusion to the calamity which not long before had befallen the city. Lightfoot argues however from another example in an earlier reign that Eusebius followed unusually good authorities about earthquakes[2] and is not unlikely, therefore, to have the right date, in which case the Roman captivity as well as the Caesarean would precede the catastrophe; and again that even on the other supposition it would not be surprising to find no allusions to the earthquake if the Epistle was written, as he supposes, quite late in the Roman captivity, i.e. some three years after the city had suffered. There is also much to be said for Hertzberg's suggestion[3] (quoted by both Lightfoot and Schiller) the two notices refer to two different earthquakes, in which case the only positive evidence for the extension of the first earthquake as far up the valley as Colossae disappears.

Of quite a different kind is the argument from καί

---

[1] *Chron.* Ol. 210 (II. p. 154 f. ed. Schöne).

[2] In the case of another earthquake of this reign, Schiller [*Nero*, 160, 172] holds that Tacitus gives the wrong year.

[3] *Geschichte Griechenlands unter der Herrschaft der Römer* II. p. 96 n. (ed. 1868).

in Eph. vi. 21, ἵνα δὲ εἰδῆτε καὶ ὑμεῖς. This it is said must mean "you as well as the Colossians," implying that the Colossians had received this knowledge first, which would imply that Tychicus went from East to West, not vice versa. But it is really inconceivable that an allusion should be made to the Epistle to the Colossians in this faint unintelligible way, and not likely that in a letter to the Ephesians, much less to a great body of Churches, such a reference should be made to little Colossae. A far more natural meaning would be "you in the recesses of Provincial Asia, as well as the brethren at Rome or in constant intercourse with Rome."

We need hardly dwell on the suggestion that had Tychicus and Onesimus been travelling from the West, the Epistle to the Ephesians must have contained a special commendation of Onesimus; or again that Onesimus as a runaway slave was more likely to expect to escape detection at Caesarea than at Rome. This is a point on which no guessing can be worth much; but if one is to guess, the miscellaneous swarms that thronged Rome would seem to offer exceptional chances of escaping detection.

A more tangible subject is the comparative opportunities of the two captivities for the conversion of Onesimus. In some way or other the runaway slave had been brought into contact with the imprisoned apostle, and learned from him the Christian faith. The words to Philemon are quite express, τοῦ ^{Philemon 10.}

ἐμοῦ τέκνου, ὃν ἐγέννησα ἐν τοῖς δεσμοῖς Ὀνήσιμον.
Now as regards Caesarea all we know of a state of
things which would make such an incident possible is
contained in Acts xxiv. 23, where we read that Felix
" gave order to the centurion that he (Paul) should be
kept in charge, and should have indulgence (ἔχειν τε
ἄνεσιν), and not to hinder any of his friends (τῶν ἰδίων
αὐτοῦ) from ministering unto him." ' Having indulgence' evidently means a less rigorous and painful
form of imprisonment, as by transference from a
noisome cell[1], and especially leave to use better food
than prison fare[2]. It is evidently such little allevia-
tions as these that are meant by the ὑπηρετεῖν of
friends[3]. This limited access of friends, for St Paul's
own relief, would not naturally introduce a heathen
runaway slave, and a heathen he must have been when
he came in contact with the imprisoned apostle.

Very different were the circumstances of the
Acts xxviii. Roman captivity as described by St Luke. On
St Paul's arrival in the city he was allowed to
v. 16. live in a private house (μένειν καθ' ἑαυτόν) "with
the soldier that guarded him." "And he abode," we
vv. 30, 31. read, "a whole space of two years in a hired lodging
of his own" (whether this μίσθωμα is or is not the same

---

[1] Passio S. Perpetuæ 3.

[2] Cf. Lightfoot's *Ignatius* i. 345 f. (ed. 1885). Also Josephus *Ant.*
xviii. 235 φυλακὴ μὲν γὰρ καὶ τήρησις ἦν μετὰ μέντοι ἀνέσεως τῆς εἰς τὴν
δίαιταν.

[3] The Syrian addition ἢ προσέρχεσθαι enlarges the sense in appearance only.

as the ξενία spoken of in the intermediate *v.* 23, is uncertain and unimportant), "and received all that went
"in unto him, preaching the Gospel of God, and
"teaching the things concerning the Lord Jesus
"Christ with all boldness, none forbidding him."
Here then was free access for any one who chose,
not for private friends only; and the opportunity
was freely used by St Paul for preaching. Under
such circumstances Onesimus might easily have
heard from others of the prisoner's wondrous dis-
course: perhaps, as Lightfoot suggests[1], he might
have known St Paul's name already, familiar as it
must have been in the ears of Philemon's household: thus he might well be led to enter one
day with the rest, and might be overcome by the
divine words which he heard. At all events Onesimus's conversion falls much more naturally into the
Roman than into the Caesarean captivity; and thereby fresh evidence is given for the conclusion involved
in the priority of the Epistle to the Philippians to
the other three, according to Lightfoot's view of their
order. Nor is there any even plausible evidence to the
contrary unless it be that of the earthquakes, which
we have seen is not really at variance with the assignation of all these letters to the Roman captivity.
How well this conclusion fits in with the contents of
the Epistle to the Ephesians, we shall see presently.

---

[1] *Colossians and Philemon*, p. 312.

The most probable year for the journey of Tychicus and the writing of the three Epistles which he carried is 63 A.D., or thereabouts; that is, late in St Paul's Roman imprisonment. In July 64 Rome was set on fire, and the persecution of Christians known by Nero's name began. It was the last period of comparative quiet before a long line of troublous days indeed.

III.

A. *External Evidence.*

THUS far we have been assuming that the Epistle was written by St Paul as it professes to be. But was it so indeed? The question having been raised by a large number of competent critics ought not to be left wholly unconsidered, though it is impossible within our limits to deal with it in any thorough manner.

It will be well to begin with looking quickly at the evidence afforded by the use of the Epistle in early writings. This does not directly touch authorship but only age. Since however most of those who dispute the genuineness of the Epistle place it in this or that generation much later than St Paul, the field of discussion may be greatly narrowed by evidence bearing on age. Of course we are concerned only with early evidence and that is almost always a little confused and vague. In due time we should get clear quotations and names of books, but by that time we should have

reached a part of the second century unimportant for
our purpose.

We begin with Clement of Rome, about 95—6 A.D.
Many passages of his have been marked as derived
from the Epistle to the Ephesians. None of them
seem to me to be quite certain, but two or three admit
of very little doubt. The strongest case perhaps is in
c. 64 ὁ ἐκλεξάμενος τὸν Κύριον Ἰησοῦν Χριστὸν καὶ
ἡμᾶς δι' αὐτοῦ εἰς λαὸν περιούσιον. The combination
ἐκλεξάμενος and εἰς λαὸν περιούσιον is probably a
reminiscence of Deuteronomy xiv. 4: but the remarkable combination of God's election of the Lord Jesus
Christ and His election of Christians into a people
for His own possession, the latter depending on the
former (ἡμᾶς δι' αὐτοῦ), looks as if it must have come
from Eph. i. 4, καθὼς ἐξελέξατο ἡμᾶς ἐν αὐτῷ κ.τ.λ.,
with an analogous διὰ Ἰησοῦ Χριστοῦ in the next
verse. The second case is in c. 46 " Have we not one
God and one Christ and one Spirit of grace which
(Spirit) was poured out upon us, and one calling in
Christ?" This passage, which is part of a warning
against strifes and divisions, if compared carefully
with Eph. iv. 4—6 will be seen to be probably
derived from it, particularly 'one calling' as repre-
senting 'one hope of your calling'; more especially
as the next sentence is " Why do we drag and rend
asunder the members of Christ, and act seditiously
toward our own body (or, the proper body, τὸ σῶμα
τὸ ἴδιον), and come to such madness that we forget

that we are *members one of another?*" (cf. Eph. iv. 25).
The other most probable coincidences are in c. 36
"Through Him *the eyes of our heart* were opened"
(cf. Eph. i. 18, where the right text is πεφωτισμένους
τοὺς ὀφθαλμοὺς τῆς καρδίας [ὑμῶν]); and in c. 38
"Let each man be subject to his neighbour" (cf.
Eph. v. 21).

We come next to Ignatius probably about fifteen
years later, i.e. roughly 110 A.D. (possibly but less
probably a few years later). First must be put aside
two or three passages which for one reason or another
might seem to be specially good evidence, but are
really irrelevant. The twelfth chapter of his Epistle
to the Ephesians ends with the sentence ὃς ἐν πάσῃ
ἐπιστολῇ μνημονεύει ὑμῶν ἐν Χριστῷ Ἰησοῦ, often rendered "in all his epistle 'to you,'" and taken as a clear
recognition of our Epistle. But this is an impossible
rendering of ἐν πάσῃ ἐπιστολῇ, and moreover, as Lightfoot says, "would be singularly unmeaning, if not un-
true," if our Epistle were meant[1]. The meaning is of
course "in every Epistle," a strange exaggeration no
doubt, but not without foundation[2]. Zahn even
goes so far as to say that the words show our
Epistle *not* to have been known to Ignatius with any
Ephesian associations: but that is too much to say.

[1] See Lightfoot, *in loco* (*The Apostolic Fathers*, Part II. vol. ii. Sect.
1, ed. 1885).
[2] See Lightfoot *l.c.* and Zahn, *Ignatius von Antiochien*, p. 607 f.
(ed. 1873).

H. R. 8

The salutation at the head of the Epistle contains
several words that seem to have been suggested by
early verses of St Paul's Epistle to the Ephesians,
though some of them appear likewise in other
Ignatian salutations: the important words are εὐλο-
γημένη, πληρώματι, προωρισμένη πρὸ αἰώνων εἶναι...
εἰς δόξαν, ἐκλελεγμένη. Further on in c. 1 the Greek
manuscript of Ignatius has a clear quotation from
Eph. v. 2 ; but late editions have rightly expelled
it on the authority of the ancient versions¹. Once
more, no reliance can be placed on τοῦ ἠγαπημένου
Ἰησοῦ Χριστοῦ in the salutation to the Smyrnaeans
notwithstanding the coincidence with ἐν τῷ ἠγαπη-
μένῳ of Eph. i. 6. This was a widely spread
designation, occurring e.g. in Clement of Rome (the
prayer in c. 59), Barnabas, and Hermas, and found
repeatedly in what are supposed to be the Christian
parts of the *Ascensio Esaiae*². It was simply an easy
alternative for the ἀγαπητός of the words spoken from
heaven at the Baptism and Transfiguration. But
when in his Epistle to Polycarp (c. 5) Ignatius enjoins
him to exhort "his brethren" to love their consorts
(συμβίους) *as the Lord the Church*, we must feel sure
that so little obvious a thought can have come only
from Eph. v. 25; and then the allusions to a Christian

---

¹ Lightfoot, *ib.* p. 31 note.
² See references of Lightfoot and Zahn (*Patr. Apost. Opera*, Fascic.
II. ed. 1876) on this passage, and Harnack on Barn. iii. 6 (*ib.* Fascic.
I. Part II. ed. 1878).

περικεφαλαία and πανοπλία in c. 6, indecisive in themselves, may be naturally referred to Eph. vi. 11, 17; and the phrases above cited from Ignatius's salutation to the Ephesians may be reasonably derived from the beginning of our Epistle.

A few months after the writings of Ignatius, comes the Epistle of Polycarp to the Philippians. Here there are more distinct quotations from the New Testament than in any previous writing, and they include two from our Epistle. Near the end of c. i. χάριτί ἐστε σεσωσμένοι, οὐκ ἐξ ἔργων must come from Eph. ii. 5, 8, 9; and in c. xii. (the Greek is lost) ut his scripturis dictum est *irascimini et nolite peccare* et *Sol non occidat super iracundiam vestram* must come from Eph. iv. 26.

The date of the Shepherd of Hermas is still an open question, but within certain limits, viz. the first forty years of the second century. It can hardly be more than a little earlier or later. The very difficult question of its use of Scripture language is best handled by Zahn in his book on Hermas[1]. The exhortations in Eph. iv. 25, 29, 30 to speak truth each with his neighbour, to let no corrupt word proceed out of the mouth, and to grieve not the Holy Spirit of God find echoes in Mand. iii. Ἀλήθειαν ἀγάπα, καὶ πᾶσα ἀλήθεια ἐκ τοῦ στόματός σου ἐκπορευέσθω, and then after a few lines μηδὲ λύπην ἐπάγειν τῷ πνεύματι τῷ σεμνῷ καὶ ἀληθεῖ; this last phrase being taken up

[1] *Der Hirt des Hermas*, pp. 412 ff. (1868).

again more precisely in Mand. x. 2, λυπεῖ τὸ πνεῦμα
τὸ ἅγιον, and several times repeated in the following
lines. Doubtless the original source is Isaiah lxiii. 10:
but there the LXX. word is παροξύνω,, while Hermas
follows St Paul in substituting λυπῶ. There is a
less clear, but still reasonably certain borrowing from
Eph. iv. 4, 5 in Sim. ix. 13, ἔσονται εἰς ἓν πνεῦμα,
καὶ ἓν σῶμα, and again (in the same chapter) ἦν
αὐτῶν ἓν πνεῦμα καὶ ἓν σῶμα [καὶ ἓν ἔνδυμα]; and four
chapters further on (c. 17) καὶ μία πίστις αὐτῶν ἐγένετο,
followed presently (cc. 17, 18) by ἓν σῶμα three times
repeated, the last time in association again with μία
πίστις. Other supposed coincidences between Hermas
and the Epistle to the Ephesians are too uncertain to
rest on.

There remains only a passage common to the
Epistle of Barnabas and to the Διδαχὴ τῶν ἀποστόλων.
Whatever be the date of the Didache as a whole, the
part of it called the Two Ways, worked up by Barnabas, is unquestionably very early. In Did. iv. 10, 11
the injunctions to masters, Οὐκ ἐπιτάξεις δούλῳ σου ἢ
παιδίσκῃ, τοῖς ἐπὶ τὸν αὐτὸν θεὸν ἐλπίζουσιν, ἐν πικρίᾳ
σου, and to servants, Ὑμεῖς δὲ οἱ δοῦλοι ὑποταγήσεσθε
τοῖς κυρίοις ὑμῶν ὡς τύπῳ θεοῦ ἐν αἰσχύνῃ καὶ φόβῳ
(Barnabas[1] has only trifling differences besides trans-
posing the precepts) are probably founded on Eph.

---

[1] c. xix. 7. His words are ὑποταγήσῃ κυρίοις ὡς τύπῳ θεοῦ ἐν
αἰσχύνῃ καὶ φόβῳ. οὐ μὴ ἐπιτάξῃς δούλῳ σου ἢ παιδίσκῃ ἐν πικρίᾳ, τοῖς
ἐπὶ τὸν αὐτὸν θεὸν ἐλπίζουσιν.

vi. 9, 5, ἀπειλή being represented by πικρία, which is
used earlier in the Epistle. In both cases the coin- Eph. iv.
cidence lies in the thoughts rather than in the 31.
words, but it is best accounted for by supposing the
Epistle to the Ephesians to have been known to the
writer.

To this evidence furnished by those who are called
the Fathers, there is little that is substantial to add
from the sadly scanty remains of those who are called
the heretics. The Epistle was evidently extant in
Marcion's time, and must have been extant some
time before him, if his Apostolicon was founded on a
previous collection of St Paul's Epistles; but this is a
disputed point, on which we have no positive evidence.
Nor do we know Marcion's own time except vaguely,
and to what period of his life the Apostolicon belongs
we do not know at all. Apparently his main activity
belongs to the latter part of the first half of the second
century. The Epistle is several times quoted in the very
interesting extracts made by Hippolytus from a book
attributed to Basilides. Basilides belongs to Hadrian's
reign, i.e. about the second or third decade of the
second century, and I fully believe those extracts to
be genuine: but some think them to have been written
by a later disciple, so that for our present purpose it
is better to leave them out of consideration. Other
quotations of the Epistle to the Ephesians in Pseudo-
Gnostical writings or extracts apparently belonging

to the latter part of the second century, may be neglected as too late to come into account.

We have now gone over all the early evidence for the existence of the Epistle to the Ephesians, and what we have found is this. In the authorities certainly belonging to the first century, Clement of Rome and the Two Ways, we have highly probable though not absolutely certain evidence. Of Hermas, a writer who may belong to any time early in the second century, much the same may be said, though here the probability almost reaches certainty. In Ignatius, probably about ten years from the beginning of the century, we find absolute certainty in one case (ὡς ὁ κύριος τὴν ἐκκλησίαν), as well as high probability in others. Lastly, in Polycarp, about the same time, there are two clear quotations which do not admit of doubt. From Barnabas and from the Didache —except the Two Ways—we obtain no evidence. Thus it is all but certain on this evidence that the Epistle to the Ephesians was in existence by about 95 A.D., quite certain that it was in existence by about fifteen years later, or conceivably a little more. Escape from this conclusion is possible only to those who treat the Epistles of Clement of Rome, Ignatius, and Polycarp as likewise spurious; and for the discussion of that question no better guide can be found than Lightfoot.

B. *Internal Evidence.*

From this preliminary survey of the external evidence bearing on possible limits for the date of the Epistle, as supplied by the traces of its use in the earlier post-biblical Christian writers, we pass to the internal evidence bearing on both its date and its authorship. It will simplify matters to begin with the more extreme views which have been entertained as to the late date implied by internal evidence : they will not detain us long. Half a century ago the prominence given to the Holy Spirit in the teaching of the Epistle, and the way in which prophets are in Eph. ii. 20, three places associated with apostles, were supposed iii. 5, iv. 11. to prove the author of the Epistle to have sympathised largely with the Montanist movement, and this would no doubt carry it a long way into the second century. Another supposed indication of Montanist influence was found in the language about the "building up of the body of Christ" c. iv. 12 f. and the "growing up to a perfect man," which was taken to reflect the Montanist idea of a fuller ripeness of the Church brought about by the Paraclete ; though there is not a trace of Montanist watchwords. Again the language about Christ and the Church was thought to be connected with the

Montanist doctrine of Monogamy; on which supposition no comment is necessary. This particular fancy soon went out of favour, as the utter incongruity between our Epistle and the Montanistic habit of mind became more apparent on consideration. As Holtzmann himself says, "With such an explanation almost all the Pauline Epistles might be Montanistic[1]."

More widely spread and more lasting has been the appeal to certain words prominent in the Epistle as derived from those whom we call Gnostics, and so suggesting a date in or about the second quarter of the second century. The most tempting of these words were πλήρωμα and αἰῶνες, both however used in senses alien to the Pseudo-Gnostical, though it is probable enough that a misunderstanding of the language of our Epistle contributed to the Pseudo-Gnostical terminology. The πολυποίκιλος σοφία ascribed to God in the Epistle was supposed to be an allusion to the varied romance of doings and sufferings attributed to the Divine Hachamoth (or Wisdom) in the Valentinian mythology. Accessory evidence to the same purport was found in the weight given to σοφία in two other places of our Epistle, though we find a similar emphasis in St Paul's earlier Epistles; and, strange to say, even in the use of the word γνῶσις in the prayer that the recipients of the Epistle might "come to know the love of Christ which is above all knowing," though in the earlier Epistles

Eph. iii. 10.

c. i. 9, 17.

c. iii. 19.

---

[1] *Kritik der Epheser- und Kolosserbrief*, p. 276 (Leipzig, 1872).

the word is freely used in a sense really nearer that which we call the Gnostic sense.

This dating of the Epistle by imagined references to Pseudo-Gnostical phraseology of the second century has still some few supporters, but has no claim to be discussed further. This cannot, however, be said of the view which has next to be considered, and which in one form or another has many able advocates. These critics recognise the absence from the Epistle of any tangible marks of the second century, but they hold that it belongs to a different and later stage of thought and feeling from that of St Paul, though it goes on the same general lines; that is, they ascribe it to an advanced disciple of St Paul rather than to the apostle himself. Such a view allows considerable latitude of dating: in accordance with it the Epistle might be almost as old as St Paul or—to take the other extreme—it might be as late as a quite early part of the second century. Then, in addition to the supposed marks of a Paulinism too advanced for St Paul, it is likewise alleged that there are marks of simply different authorship, differences of language, style and the like. And further, besides the evidence said to be afforded by the Epistle itself taken alone, appeal is made to other evidence obtained from comparison with other Epistles, that to the Colossians and the First Epistle of St Peter. All these kinds of supposed evidence have been worked out with admirable care and subtlety in a succession of recent books, such as Holtzmann's introduction to the New Testament[1] (which, however, needs to be supplemented from his earlier book on the Epistles to the Ephesians and Colossians), the new edition of Pfleiderer's *Paulinismus*[2], and the recent commentaries of Klöpper[3] and Von Soden[4].

It would be vain to attempt to set forth and examine all the particulars of the supposed evidence under these heads within the limits of these lectures. But it will be well to give some little time to those points in which either the appearance of difference is most plausible or which have otherwise most interest. If in this way we are delayed from entering on the interpretation of the opening verses of the Epistle, yet it would be a mistake to suppose that we shall be occupied exclusively with questions of Introduction. Our inquiry must inevitably include some examination of important passages of the Epistle, so that in the guise of Introduction we shall in fact be brought in contact with a succession of questions of Interpretation.

The supposed marks of a later time than St Paul's lie partly in changed circumstances presupposed in the Epistle, partly in changed doctrine as expressed

---

[1] *Lehrbuch der historisch-kritiker Einleitung in das Neue Testament.* Freiburg, 1892 (3te Auflage).

[2] *Der Paulinismus.* Leipzig, 1890.

[3] *Der Brief an die Epheser.* Göttingen, 1891.

[4] In Holtzmann's *Handcommentar zum Neuen Testament*, Band III., Freiburg, 1891.

in the Epistle itself. The two cannot, however, be kept apart; for evidently a change of circumstances might in itself quite naturally lead to a change in at least the proportion and mode of expression of doctrine. What then are the facts? First, to speak in quite general terms, no one who carefully reads the Epistle to the Ephesians can doubt that its doctrinal contents do differ considerably from those of any one of St Paul's earlier Epistles, or of all of them taken together. But that proves little. What we really have to ask is whether the differences are morally incompatible with identity of authorship.

Now it seems tolerably obvious that a great theological teacher, such as St Paul confessedly was, in writing to different Churches under different circumstances would naturally be led to lay stress on different parts of the sum total of his belief; so that at one time this, at one time that doctrine or aspect of doctrine might be expected to fall into subordination or to be altogether unnoticed. And we have an additional assurance that it would be so in the fact that in the Epistle to the Romans St Paul shows, to say the least, how catholic-minded he was, how little disposed to measure truth by a monotonous partisan standard.

All this would hold good supposing his own thoughts and beliefs to have remained stationary from the time he went forth from Antioch till his death. But that is most unlikely. A mind like his,

in constant living contact with truth, needing and
receiving fresh enlightenment from day to day, for
dealing with new and changing needs of the Churches,
must assuredly have known growth. New experience
must have brought new light, giving comparatively
clear vision of truths hitherto imperfectly grasped or
even overlooked altogether, and often changing the
relative importance of truths already familiar. And,
supposing such a growth to have arisen, it would be
strange if it left no traces in the extant Epistles of
different dates. The supposition does no injury to
their authority as books of Scripture ; it only helps to
wean us from the delusively and unreally simple
habit of using them as detached oracles, and helps
us to understand better the manifoldness of truth
through their manifold adaptation in respect of time
and place and circumstance.

It would therefore be unreasonable to take the
presence of new doctrinal ideas, or a new proportion
among earlier doctrinal ideas, as evidence of different
authorship, unless there be a real want of harmony
between the later and the earlier teaching, and unless
the later way of thinking and speaking cannot be
easily conceived as a natural outgrowth of the earlier
in the case of a single man, and that such a
man as we know St Paul to have been. It is
agreed on both sides that this is a case of natural
outgrowth ; so that the question is simply whether it
is such a natural outgrowth as can be reasonably

attributed to the apostle himself under changing circumstances, or such as must be due to two different minds, the younger being however united to the elder by bonds of intimate and sympathetic discipleship, doctrinal if not personal.

Let us now look a little at some of the chief combinations of identity and difference between St Paul's earlier recorded theology and that of the Epistle to the Ephesians. Pfleiderer's chapter[1] on the Epistle will conveniently bring to our notice the questions raised by a temperate and careful opponent of its genuineness. We may begin with the relation of Jews to Gentiles as Christians. In the Epistles to the Galatians and Romans, and especially in the former, we have records of St Paul's efforts to maintain for Christian converts from heathenism a place within the Christian fold wholly equal with that held by converts of Jewish birth. Here in the Epistle to the Ephesians the assured position of the Gentile Christians is simply taken for granted. Nay, while it is they that stand in the foreground of the Epistle, they are taught to recognise and revere the privileges granted by God to the old Israel in the old time, and to cultivate brotherhood with the living Christian heirs of those now superseded prerogatives. This union of complete rejection of exclusive Jewish claims on behalf of Law or circumcision with earnest insistence on the divine calling of Israel as

[1] *Der Paulinismus* II. c. 3.

the foundation of the Christian calling for Jew and
Gentile alike, is entirely in the spirit of the Epistle
to the Romans. Only the stress, so to speak, is shifted,
because the circumstances have shifted, as Pfleiderer
fully allows. The difference, it is truly said, lies in
the clearness and emphasis with which the idea of
Catholicity, that is to say universality, is in this
Epistle for the first time put forward, in the spirit
of the Fourth Gospel. The duty of Jewish and Gentile
fellowship is here deduced from the eternal purpose
of God and the very idea of the Christian faith, not,
as in earlier Epistles, from arguments about the
Law and the Promise. Yet again this is only the
teaching of the Epistle to the Romans a little more
unfolded. Those arguments about Law and Promise
have their proper place in a refutation of Jewish
exclusive claims such as was in place in the early
chapters of that Epistle, but would have been out of
place in the Epistle to the Ephesians. Moreover St
Paul regards them as themselves part of the evidence
for the true nature of God's all-embracing purposes
for the whole human race which are set forth in the
Epistle to the Ephesians, but set forth also implicitly
in Rom. ix—xi. and in the final Doxology ; to say
nothing of the far-reaching, but often forgotten, significance of the words πᾶς, πάντες, which may
almost be called the keywords of that Epistle.

Once more, in both Epistles alike, though in
different language, the need for the universal salva-

tion is made to rest on the universality of the previous
corruption. In Eph. ii. 1—3 the reference to the
previous Gentile corruption is emphatically followed
up by an assertion of a corresponding Jewish corruption (καὶ ὑμᾶς ὄντας νεκρούς....ἐν οἷς καὶ ἡμεῖς
πάντες ἀνεστράφημέν ποτε and especially καὶ ἤμεθα
τέκνα φύσει ὀργῆς ὡς καὶ οἱ λοιποί). This exactly
answers to the way in which the terrible indictment
of heathendom in Rom. i. 18—fin. is followed up by
the condemnation of the Jews in ii. 17—fin., and both
are placed on a level in this respect in iii. 9 and elsewhere. It is said indeed that the Epistle to the Ephesians differs from the earlier Epistles by its language
about the Gentiles having been "far off." But the Eph. ii. 13,
phrase came in most naturally with the reminiscence ^{17.}
of the language of Isaiah lvii. 19; lii. 7, and was in
itself a natural way of expressing an obvious fact;
which in like manner is in Rom. xi. for another
purpose expressed by the much less obvious image
of the wild olive tree.

Again it is said that, by a divergence in the opposite direction, the Epistle to the Ephesians speaks
of circumcision not simply as obsolete but as in itself
contemptible, in a way that St Paul's writings never
do. The passage is c. ii. 11, ὑμεῖς τὰ ἔθνη ἐν σαρκί,
οἱ λεγόμενοι ἀκροβυστία ὑπὸ τῆς λεγομένης περιτομῆς
ἐν σαρκὶ χειροποιήτου. Here λεγομένης, the word that
gives offence, is called forth in answer to the preceding
λεγόμενοι; and its sense, 'so called circumcision,' so far

from being un-Pauline, is (taken by itself) a paradox, which is at once explained when we remember the language of Rom. ii. 28 f., where the circumcision which is ἐν τῷ φανερῷ ἐν σαρκί is pronounced to be not the true circumcision, which title belongs only to circumcision of heart.

This view of the parallelism, so to speak, of Jew and Gentile and the equal union of both in Christ leads us to another great and prominent head of the distinctive teaching of our Epistle, its teaching about *the Church.* Here for the first time, we hear Christians throughout the world described as together making up a single Ecclesia, i.e., assembly of God, or Church ; and here for the first time we find the relation of Christ to *the* or *a* Church conceived as that of a Head to the Body. But these novelties of thought and language stand in the closest connexion with what preceded. The union of Jew and Gentile in a single undivided society, on the basis of their one and identical standing before God and their one faith in the one Lord, itself constituted a single universal people of God ; and this, as we have seen, was just what was involved in the teaching of the Epistle to the Romans.

Another impulse towards laying stress on the unity of the society of Christians throughout the world doubtless came from the position of St Paul as writing from Rome. The eagerness with which, as we see from the Acts of the Apostles and the Epistle to the Romans, he had looked forward to personal converse with the Roman Church after carrying the Gentile collection as a token of brotherhood to Jerusalem, arose out of a feeling that so a completeness would be divinely given to his own work as the herald of the Gospel to the Gentiles, by his presence in the centre of the Gentile world. That hope had been long delayed by imprisonment : but now at last St Paul found himself at Rome, manifestly brought thither by the hand of God. With everything there reminding him of the external unity of the Empire, it could not be strange if his surroundings added force to his thought of a still more comprehensive unity resting on faith in the unseen Lord.

Nor again would it be strange that he should use the name Ecclesia in this new and extended sense, although hitherto it had been applied only to the Christian community of Jerusalem or Judea, or to individual local Christian communities outside the Holy Land. That early Christian community of Palestine, when as yet there were none in Gentile lands, had rightly appropriated to themselves this name of Israel, not improbably guided thereto by our Lord's words to St Peter; and now, when there was living in many lands such a varied multitude of those who, in St Paul's own phrase addressed to the Corinthians, "called upon the name of our Lord 1 Cor. i. 2. Jesus Christ in every place," nothing was more natural than that St Paul should gather them to-

gether under that one ancient name Ecclesia, believing
as he did that they all were members of God's true
Israel.

As an argument against the Pauline origin of our
Epistle, it is urged by some that this insistence on the
unity of the Church is the mark of a much later time
when the churches of different lands were drawing
closer together in resistance to common dangers, and
binding themselves together by a single organisation.
This however is to misunderstand the Epistle altogether. The unity of which it speaks has in itself
nothing to do with organisation, though no doubt a
sense of it might be expected to help towards the
growth of organisation. The units of the one Church
spoken of in the Epistle are not churches but individual
men. From the first, each Christian community as
soon as it was formed became as it were a school by
which its members were trained in the life of mutual
fellowship. Thus in St Paul's earlier Epistles, but
with greater distinctness in the Epistle to the Ephesians, each Christian was taught to recognise the
bonds which joined him to every other Christian
throughout the world, and the debt of love and
helpfulness which he owed in some manner to each
and all. This teaching is entirely in St Paul's own
spirit; and it has no trace of such words or thoughts
as must have inevitably accompanied the setting forth
of an external unity. The society was in this sense
external, that membership of it was constituted by

the external act of baptism and the accompanying
public profession of faith : but the unity of this society
was itself invisible, believed in by Christians but
hidden from all who did not worship the unseen
Lord.

Another new characteristic in the language used
about the Church in our Epistle is the representation
of Christ as the Head of the Body. The image of
a body as expressive of the relations between the
members of a society of men was old enough, being
found in Greek Stoics. St Paul not only gave special
force to it, but raised it into a higher sphere by connecting it with the relations of men to the Lord
Himself. In the earlier Epistles, however, He is not
spoken of as the Head of the Body. In Rom. xii. 4, 5
we read "Even as we have many members in one
" body, and all the members have not the same office
" (or action), so we, who are many, are one body in
" Christ, and severally members one of another." Here
Christ appears as the bond or uniting element by
which the multitude of individual men became a
body : but the wide range of sense in which the
pregnant phrase "in Christ" is used by St Paul,
leaves it undetermined whether Christ Himself was
regarded as having, so to speak, a place within the
imagery of the body and its members. In 1 Cor. xii.
the language is apparently more definite but more
peculiar: "as the body is one, and hath many 1 Cor. xii.
members, and all the members of the body, being 12.

many, are one body, so also *is Christ*: "—not "so are we in Christ," but so "is Christ," i.e., He Himself is in some sense identified with the Christian body as made up of many members. Later on in the chapter we have the more familiar language "Now ye are a body of Christ, and severally members," where still there is nothing to suggest that Christ's relation to the body is that of head to the other members, and moreover in the words " Again the head [cannot say to the feet] I have no need of you " the head appears simply as one member among many.

But though the language of Eph. i. 22, iv. 15 f. (which is also the language of Col. i. 18) is thus new, it was perfectly natural for St Paul himself to use. He had already employed the image of a head in an analogous though possibly not identical manner in a very remarkable verse of his first Epistle to the Corinthians, "Now I would have you know that the head of every man (ἀνδρός—man as distinct from woman) is Christ, and the head of a woman is the man (her husband), and the head of Christ is God." We must not stop to enquire into the exact force of headship in each of these three clauses, or in all. It is likely enough that the large range of meaning attaching to the Hebrew *rôsh* enabled St Paul to stretch as it were the meaning of the Greek κεφαλή. But the presence of the article before κεφαλή in the first clause, together with the insertion of παντός before ἀνδρός, in contrast to the absence

1 Cor. xii. 27.

ib. 21.

1 Cor. xi. 3.

of ἡ in the second and third clauses, and of πάσης
in the second, suggests that it is as one out of many,
as member of a body, that a man is spoken of as
having Christ for his Head. And again in the second
clause what is said of a husband as head of his wife
is a distinct anticipation of Eph. v. 23, where the two
headships are brought expressly together.

Another quite different antecedent of the idea of
Christ's relation to the Church as Head, as we find it
in the Epistle to the Ephesians, may safely be
recognised in the association of the image of a
building with that of a body as together shadow-
ing forth the nature of the Christian fellowship,
each being as it were complementary to the other.
One who can look on Christ as the Cornerstone
of the Temple not made with hands, would almost
of necessity look upon Him likewise as the Head
of the Body, even if he did not find a connecting
link in the phrase '*Head* of the Corner' by which
the fundamental Psalm, Ps. 118, described the Cornerstone. Now it is true we have no direct evidence from St Paul's earlier epistles that the image
of the Cornerstone was familiar to his mind. But
if we remember that this image came from Our
Lord's own implicit appropriation of the words
of the Psalm to Himself in the parable of the _{Mt. xxi.}
Wicked Husbandmen recorded in all the first three _{42, Mk xii.
10, 11,}
Gospels, not to speak of St Peter's reference to it _{Lk. xx. 17.}
before the Sanhedrim as well as afterwards in his _{Acts iv. 11.}

1 Pet. ii.4 f. epistle, it must be impossible for us to believe that the idea was either unknown to St Paul from the day that he became a Christian, or was rejected by him. On these then, as on other grounds, the negative fact that Christ is not called Head of the Church in the earlier Epistles, has no force towards shewing that this Epistle must have a different author.

We come next, by an easy transition, to the differences of the Epistle to the Ephesians from the earlier Epistles on the Person and Office of the Lord Himself, i.e., in what is now commonly known as Christology. Difficult as it may be to determine precisely the range of St Paul's belief on this central subject as implied in his earlier Epistles, it is at least clear that to his mind our Lord's human birth was no absolute beginning of existence, but, to use the image supplied to us by St John's Gospel, a descent from heaven. This is implied not only in the great passage of Phil. ii., but in the corresponding earlier language of 2 Cor. viii. 9 "how for your sakes he became poor, when he was rich" (δι' ὑμᾶς ἐπτώ-χευσεν πλούσιος ὤν). So also Gal. iv. 4 "God sent forth His Son, born of a woman, born under law, &c." and the similar Rom. viii. 3 "God sending His own Son in the likeness of flesh of sin &c." where the accompanying words exclude the supposition that St Paul meant a Sonship coming into existence only with the sending.

But in the Epistle to the Ephesians and still

more in that to the Colossians much more than
this is said. The Lordship of Christ is extended
from men to the whole created world, visible and
invisible, and carried back to the very beginning
of things. In Col. i. 16 f. we are told explicitly
that " in Him were all things created in the heavens
" and upon the earth, things visible and things in-
" visible,......all things have been created through
" Him and unto Him; and He is before all things
" and in Him all things consist." In the Epistle to
the Ephesians there is no clear reference to this pri-
mordial relation of Christ to the Universe; but all
things in heaven as well as earth are represented as Eph. i. 10.
sharing in the reconciliation effected by His death.
In this Epistle the prominent subject is that Headship
to the Ecclesia which likewise not only has a place in
the Epistle to the Colossians, but stands there just
after the words quoted above "And He is the Head of Col. i. 18 f.
"the Body, the Ecclesia, Who is the beginning, the first-
" born from the dead, that He might in all things be
" Himself the First." But in our Epistle the foundation
of this Headship of the Ecclesia is represented as laid
in the very beginning of things. Membership of the
Body is referred back to God's own election, and this
again is apparently made to rest on a corresponding
direction of the divine Will towards Christ Himself
before all human history. God's *present* blessing of Eph. iii.
Christians in all spiritual blessings in the heavenly 14.
world in Christ is put in express parallelism with His

having chosen them from the first,—"even as He chose us *in Him* before the foundation of the world." So also the full force of the language of the sixth and ninth verses of the first chapter implies that "*in* Christ," "*in* the Father's Beloved," and in the Father's mind towards Him, were implicitly involved, so to speak, from before the Creation the many sons who after long ages should by adoption be taken as it were into Him.

But though language of this kind is absent from the earlier epistles, they are not wanting in other language which at least points in the same direction. Both the primary relation of the universe to Christ and specially the relation of the Ecclesia to Him are involved in 1 Cor. viii. 6; "to us there is one God, "the Father, from (or out of) Whom are all things, and "we unto (or into) Him; and one Lord, Jesus Christ, "*through whom* are *all things*, and *we* through Him." The connecting link between these two Headships, that of the universe and that of the Ecclesia, is the Headship of mankind: and of this there are intimations in the earlier Epistles, viz. in the replacement of Adam by Christ as the last or second Adam, i.e. as the true Head of the whole human race (so 1 Cor. xv. 45—49, compare also 22; Rom. v. 14, Ἀδάμ, ὅς ἐστι τύπος τοῦ μέλλοντος).

Again it is undeniably true that in the Epistle to the Ephesians Christ is spoken of as the agent in certain Divine acts in which the earlier Epistles

and that to the Colossians speak of God or the
Father as the agent.   In Col. i. 19, He Whose good
pleasure it was that in Christ should all the πλήρωμα
dwell, i.e., the Father, is said to have through Him
reconciled all things into Him ; perhaps also it is the
Father that is said in the next clause to have made
peace by the blood of His Cross.   This is the usual
and the prima facie interpretation, though a quite
possible punctuation would favour the alternative
view¹.   Still more uncertain is the subject of the
verb ἀποκατήλλαξεν (if that is the right reading)
in verse 21 ; and there is an analogous ambiguity in
Col. ii. 13 f.², preceded as this difficult passage is by
a sentence of which God is clearly the subject, and
followed by one in which Christ is clearly the subject.
But in 2 Cor. v. 18 f. there can be no doubt that it
is God Himself who appears as the Reconciler of
men to Himself "through Christ."   In Eph. ii. 16 on
the other hand it is Christ who appears as the
Reconciler, reconciling both Israel and the Gentiles
(τοὺς ἀμφοτέρους) in one body to God through the
Cross.   No competent person probably would say
that the two modes of speech are *contradictory :* but,

---

¹ Put ὅτι ἐν αὐτῷ—εἰς αὐτόν into a parenthesis, so joining εἰρηνοποιήσας to the clause ending with πρωτεύων, this arrangement requires
the (quite possible) omission of the second δι' αὐτοῦ, and the assignment
of a virtually transitive force to εἰρηνοποιήσας with a sense nearly
equivalent to that involved in ἀποκαταλλάξαι.

² Put καὶ ὑμᾶς—σὺν αὐτῷ (or possibly παραπτώματα) into a parenthesis.

though not contradictory, are they so different in conception as to suggest different authorship? I cannot think so. The language of the Second Epistle to the Corinthians answers to what one may call St Paul's normal theology, in which the Father is set before us as the primary agent in all the economy of salvation, the Son as the intermediate agent or instrument [this thought is commonly expressed by διά with the genitive], through whom the Father's action takes effect. But nowhere in St Paul's writings are we led to think of Christ as a mere instrument: He is always the living Son, gladly fulfilling the living Father's Will. It is moreover worth notice

Col. iii. 13. that in the Epistle to the Colossians "the Lord" (v. l. "the Christ": doubtless Christ is meant in either case) appears as forgiving (ἐχαρίσατο) men their

Eph. iv. 32. offences, while in that to the Ephesians the forgiveness (again ἐχαρίσατο) is ascribed to "God in Christ": i.e. the variation of language is inverted. We have no reason therefore to think that another than St Paul must be speaking to us when we read a passage in which the ultimate agency of the Father is passed over in silence, and the one agent named is Christ. The motive for this less usual way of speaking is easily seen if we read carefully the whole of Eph. ii. 11—22 on the admission of the Gentiles to a share in the Messiah of Israel. The middle sentence, vv. 14—18, beginning "For Himself is our Peace," and ending "because through Him we both have our access in

one Spirit unto the Father," would most naturally
keep Him as its subject throughout, and lay the
stress on His share in the work of reconciliation,
unless to do so were felt to be a departure from
truth.

So again it is urged that while in 1 Cor. xii. 28
the various functions and gifts in the Church are
referred to God as their author, in Eph. iv. 11 a
similar office is assigned to Christ. Doubtless the
fact is so; but the difference of contexts at once
explains it. In 1 Cor. xii. St Paul is expounding the
relation of the body to its several members as a
divine ordinance (a part of creation, so to speak), the
special collocation and function of each being arranged
by Him (ἔθετο v. 18). And so, when in v. 28 he
comes down to the concrete functions and gifts of
actual Churches, he repeats that they too owe their
several places to the discriminating purpose of God
(again ἔθετο ὁ θεός). In Eph. iv. on the contrary
St Paul is speaking of the gifts which Christ sent
down when He had ascended up on high, the
historical fulfilment, as it were, of the original purpose.
His starting point is the quotation from Psalm lxviii., Eph. iv. 8;
or rather from a Christian adaptation of it, with Ps. lxviii.
'*given*' substituted for '*received*' ("when He ascended 18.
on high, He led captivity captive, and *gave* gifts to
men "): and when, three verses further on, he proceeds
"And Himself gave some apostles, some prophets &c.,"
the word 'gave' (ἔδωκεν) is caught up from the 'gave'

in the modified Psalm, and thus brought into close connexion with the results of the Ascension. But there is nothing unnatural in supposing that the same writer might, when writing from these two different points of view, in the one case ascribe the agency to God, in the other to Christ.

The high improbability that these various differences of language are due to difference of theology is shewn by the emphasis with which the subordination of the Son to the Father is implied in i. 17 ("the God of our Lord Jesus Christ"), not to speak of the various important passages in which God Himself stands at the head as Himself the doer of deeds

Eph. i. 3—6, 8—11, 17—23; ii. 4—10; iii. 9—11, 14—21; cp. iv. 6; v. 20.

of blessing for men. The two sides of the truth with which we are now dealing are brought together in strict conformity with St Paul's acknowledged teaching, in iv. 32 — v. 2 (where the sense is obscured by making a new chapter or section), "Forgiving each other, even as *God* also *in Christ* forgave you. Be ye therefore imitators *of God* [not of Christ], as beloved children; and walk in love, as Christ also loved you, and gave Himself up for you, an offering and a sacrifice to God for an odour of a sweet smell."

cp. Rom. v. 5—11; viii. 32—39.

Another alleged indication of different authorship for this Epistle is the prominence given to the Holy Spirit. Doubtless the contrast with the Epistle to the Colossians is great in this respect; but there is

no similar contrast with the earlier epistles, especially
with the Epistle to the Romans and the First Epistle
to the Corinthians. The critic who dwells on the
supposed peculiarity himself rightly associates it with
the prominence given to the Ecclesia in the Epistle
to the Ephesians, and thus suggests the true answer.
In the First Epistle to the Corinthians and in that to
the Ephesians alike St Paul is anxiously insisting on
the mutual duties of members of the Christian
community, and therefore has need to go back to the
inner principle of its life, the one uniting Spirit.
Only in the First Epistle to the Corinthians he is
dealing with the Ecclesia of a single city, the members
of which were in constant converse with each other;
in the Epistle to the Ephesians he is dealing with the
universal Ecclesia, the members of which were scat-
tered through many lands, so that the hidden bonds
of fellowship between them were only too liable to
be forgotten: and thus the language in which the
Spirit is set forth as an object for faith takes
naturally a higher flight in the latter case than in
the former.

A more really significant change perhaps than any
of these is a change in the tone of speaking about the
present and the future. The immediate imminence
of the Coming of the Lord has faded out of view; the
anticipation of it seems now to include a sense of its
possible remoteness. No stress can rightly be laid on

the passage chiefly cited to shew that the Epistle to
the Ephesians has the thought of Christian men as
Eph. ii. 6. already in heaven while here on earth (καὶ συνήγειρεν
καὶ συνεκάθισεν ἐν τοῖς ἐπουρανίοις ἐν Χριστῷ Ἰησοῦ),
the reference being to the Ascension as implicitly
involving for the members what was confessedly true
for the Head.   But the sense of present blessedness
Eph. iv.
11—16. does pervade the Epistle; and moreover what is said
on the purposes of the bestowal of the gifts of Christ
from above suggests, to say the least, the image of a
long and gradual growth reaching far out into the
future from age to age, consisting partly in the per-
fecting of the Christian community and its members,
partly (I cannot but think, though this is not
explicitly written) in the gathering together of the
human race into this its true and proper community,
through knowledge of the Son of God in accordance
with the purpose of that Gospel to the nations of
which so much is said in the Epistle.   But nothing
was more natural than that a change like this should
come over St Paul's mind, when year after year
passed away, and still there was no sign of the Lord's
coming, and when the spread of the faith through the
Roman Empire, and the results which it was producing, would give force to all such ways of thinking
as are represented by the image of the leaven
leavening the lump.   In the earlier Epistles themselves there is a certain gradation in this respect from
the earliest extant, the two to the Thessalonians,

onwards to that to the Romans. That reflexion on
God's ordering of the ages of the human past which
leaves so deep a mark on the last-named Epistle,
and which reappears in other language in that
to the Ephesians, might easily suggest the thought
that perhaps a long human future still remained,
to be drawn out and governed by the same divine
counsel. It is on the strength of an appeal in
chapter iii. to what God had purposed and done in
the ages of the past that at the end of the chapter
the doxology breaks forth, "To Him that is able to
do exceeding abundantly above all that we ask or
think, according to the power that is made to work
in us, to Him be the glory in the Ecclesia and in
Christ Jesus unto all generations of the age of the
ages."

Another point, supposed to be unfavourable to
St Paul's authorship, is the manner in which "the
apostles" are twice spoken of, "built upon the Eph. ii. 20.
foundation of the apostles and prophets," and "revealed to His holy apostles and prophets in [the] Eph. iii. 5.
Spirit." In so far as the incongruity is thought to
arise from a fundamental and permanent opposition
between St Paul and the Twelve, it would be
evidently impossible to discuss so vast a question
now. But it is worth while to notice how short-
sighted it would be to deduce the true nature of
St Paul's relations with the Twelve from certain well-

known language about the Twelve employed in the
Epistle to the Galatians and the Second Epistle to
the Corinthians. That language was wholly defen-
sive: its purpose was not to impugn the apostolic
authority of the Twelve, but to vindicate St Paul's
own against men who, by claiming for the Twelve
an exclusive apostolicity, were striving to undermine
St Paul's position and undo his work. But the
true apostolicity of the Twelve was not, and could
not be, doubted by St Paul: indeed it is assumed in
his vindication of his own title to call himself an
apostle, i.e. to be as one of them.

Nor again is there a word in his earlier epistles
which suggests that the Twelve even at that time
objected to the terms on which he preached the
Gospel to the Gentiles: nay, the contrary is implied
in the verses that come between that very passage
from which we learn of the temporary hesitation of
some of the Twelve and that other passage which
records St Peter's equally temporary cowardice at
Antioch. This evidence too is independent of the
explicit account in Acts xv., the trustworthiness of
which is questioned by many, on plausible but quite
insufficient grounds. And if this was the attitude
of the Twelve to St Paul at the time of his second
missionary journey, still more was it likely that they
would recognise his Gospel to the Gentiles as in
a special manner owned by God at this later time
when Eastern Europe as well as Western Asia

Gal. ii.
7—10.

abounded in churches in large measure of heathen origin.

We need not discuss now whether the 'prophets' here mentioned were or were not, wholly or in part, identical with the 'apostles.' Thus much is certain, that the two names represent the two types of guidance specially given to that earliest age; that of apostles, as eyewitnesses of the Lord's own life, death, and resurrection, and that of prophets, as receivers of special present monitions from the Holy Spirit. We learn from the Acts of the Apostles the part played by these prophetic monitions in the recognition of fresh steps in the expansion of church membership as divinely ordained, the most striking example being that of the original Antiochian mission of Paul and Barnabas. Thus the phrase about its having been Acts xiii. in that latest generation 'revealed to Christ's holy [1—4.] apostles and prophets in [the] Spirit that the Gentiles are fellow-heirs' does but sum up in a pregnant form what had been the real course of things.

Nor is any additional difficulty created, as some think, by the epithet 'holy,' which it is said would naturally be used only by a writer of the next or a later generation, to whom the apostles were venerated figures of the past. Doubtless this would be a natural origin for the epithet: but a not less natural one would be St Paul's sense of the peculiarly consecrated function which apostles and prophets had to discharge for the whole body of ἅγιοι (cp. Luke i. 70 τῶν ἁγίων

H. R.   10

ἀπ᾽ αἰῶνος προφητῶν αὐτοῦ). Such an usage would be exactly like his use of κλητός for himself in association

Rom. i. 1, 6 f.; 1 Cor. i. 1, 2.

with a church of κλητοί. Every one will feel how incongruous it would have been as a matter of language for him to speak of himself directly and individually as 'holy': but the incongruity vanishes when he merges himself in the body of apostles, and in his usage the conceptions of *calledness* (so to speak) and holiness are nearly connected.

This passage which we have been examining, so understood, shews in its turn how fitly in the twin passage St Paul himself could speak of the Gentiles now admitted to be of the household of God as

Eph. ii. 20.

"built upon the foundation of the Apostles and prophets." He had in mind the historical order of the actual structure and growth of the Ecclesia itself, not any authority over the Ecclesia. The foundation itself, the lowest course of living stones (as St Peter would say), consisted of those who had been chosen to look upon the Lord in His human manifestation and bear witness of what they had beheld, and of those who had been chosen to be the utterers of special voices of the Spirit. To them were added, and on them were built up as fresh members of their community, the multitudes, first of Jews, then also of Gentiles, who believed through their word. It matters little that this precise conception is without parallel in St Paul's earlier Epistles. Given that his purpose was to bring out the various privileges to which Gentile

Christians had been admitted, and that in connexion with the general image of a building inhabited by God,—an image of which he makes ample use elsewhere, but which was of special value to him for the purposes of this Epistle—then the special image of the foundation would be at once a natural and a vivid way of setting forth the true historic basis on which Gentile no less than Jewish Christendom rested. Nor would he by so using it, as some say, contradict as it were the image employed by himself in 1 Cor. iii. 10 ff., where it is said that "other foundation can no man lay but that which is laid, which is Jesus Christ," for there he is not speaking of the Christian society, but the Christian faith: what is there spoken of as built on the foundation is not men but teachings or ways of life. Nor in the Epistle to the Ephesians is there reason to doubt that the cornerstone is itself part of the foundation.

Once more, the *prima facie* singularity of that twice repeated phrase about apostles and prophets disappears when we observe that in this same chapter Eph. iv. apostles and prophets stand first in the list of gifts 11. given to men by the ascended Christ, these two and these alone having unique and exceptional functions of direct divine origin, needed for the exceptional wants of the apostolic age. And this is not all, for they stand in a precisely similar manner at the head of that analogous list of representative orderings by God of members of a body which came before us a little while ago in 1 Cor. xii.[1] Thus the *prima facie* peculiarity of the phrase as it occurs in the two first passages is entirely removed.

From the language of the Epistle about the apostles as a body we pass naturally to its language about St Paul himself, which is in like manner said to be unfavourable to his authorship. It is thought strange and forced that St Paul should dwell thus emphatically on the special charge received by him from God towards the Gentiles. It would perhaps be enough to point in reply to language implying the same charge, if less elaborate in wording, in earlier Epistles, as Rom. xi. 13; xv. 16, and several verses of the Epistle to the Galatians. But there is still stronger, if less obvious, justification, supposing that any justification be needed, for such language as coming from St Paul writing at Rome to the Christians of Western Asia Minor. To two temptations in particular these mainly Gentile churches would after a time be exposed, first to sit loose to all fellowship with Jewish Christians and to the historic basis of the Christian faith as laid in Israel; and secondly to misuse the freedom from the Jewish Law, making it into an excuse for a free and easy kind of Christianity, somewhat negligent, to say the least, of common duties towards God and man, even towards the brethren. A large part of the Epistle is virtually a

Eph. iii. 1—3, 7; iv. 1; vi. 20.

---

[1] See page 139.

solemn exhortation on these two heads, and there was
every reason why St Paul in thus writing should appeal
to the special right which he had to give the warning,
he the divinely appointed champion of Gentile freedom, and now a prisoner owing to his labours in that
cause.

It is hardly credible that this language, vindicating
St Paul's claim to be listened to by Gentile Christians,
should have been thought to make unreal those other
words in iii. 8, "to me, who am less than the least of
all saints, was this grace given," words which are
accordingly treated as a clumsy exaggeration of what
the true St Paul had written to the Corinthians 1 Cor. xv.
about being 'the least of the apostles, not meet to 9.
be called an apostle.' There the range of comparison
is limited by the context, here there was no ground
for stopping short of "all saints." In striving to
bring the Asiatic Christians to a true sense of the
greatness of the grace of God shewn to them, he
speaks in the power of his own deep sense of the
greatness of the grace of God shewn to himself. The
individual unworthiness does but lift higher his calling
as the apostle of the Gentiles. Nay, the combination
and contrast of the individual unworthiness and the
divine calling are explicitly set forth in the most
obviously Pauline of the early Epistles, that to the Gal. i.
Galatians. 13—16.

More plausible is the appeal to Eph. iii. 2—4, a
difficult passage, at all events at first sight. The

expression of an assurance that the recipients of the letter, as they read it, would be able to appreciate the writer's understanding in the mystery of the Christ is said to be an awkward way of cultivating assent, unworthy (I suppose it is meant) of St Paul's dignified directness. Nor is it to be denied that there is something unusual and obscure in the language used if, as is generally if not universally assumed, the " reading" (ἀναγινώσκοντες) anticipated for the recipients of the Epistle means reading of the Epistle itself, or of some part of it. Yet even so the evidence against St Paul's authorship would be trivial and untrustworthy, taken by itself: for nothing is more characteristic of St Paul than to use language modified by undercurrents of thought or feeling which are not at all obvious to trace. My own impression, however, is that the reading spoken of is not of the Epistle, but of the prophetic parts of the Old Testament. Such, I am convinced, is the meaning in that remarkable phrase of Mat. xxiv. 15, ‖ Mark xiii. 14, ὁ ἀναγινώσκων νοείτω[1]. There is no force in what is commonly said against this interpretation of our first two Gospels, that in St Mark no mention is made of Daniel, the prophet supposed to be read; for even without his name so remarkable a phrase as that translated "the abomination of desolation" would at

---

[1] We have the same combination here δύνασθε ἀναγινώσκοντες νοῆσαι. It occurs again in Origen *de Principiis* iv. quoted in *Philocalia* i. 8 τῆς ἀναγνώσεως καὶ νοήσεως of the Scriptures.

once bring to mind the book from which it was taken.
But both in the Gospels and here the absolute use of
the word *read* in the sense of reading Scripture was
apparently in conformity with Jewish usage, as may
be seen by various examples given under קָרָא and
its derivatives in Levy and Fleischer's Lexicon[1],
and that in the case of both reading aloud and
silent reading. This use is apparently confirmed by
the absolute use of τῇ ἀναγνώσει in 1 Tim. iv. 13,
and the similar absolute use of ἀνάγνωσμα in the
early Fathers (e.g. Origen *Cels.* iii. 50). This interpretation of ἀναγινώσκοντες in Eph. iii. 4 gives force
to the otherwise obscure πρὸς ὃ which precedes.
The recipients of the Epistle were to perceive St
Paul's understanding in the mystery of Christ not
simply by reading his exposition, but by keeping
it in mind when they read ancient prophecy, com-
paring the one with the other. Thus the sense
answers exactly to the sense of the phrase "by
prophetic scriptures" (διὰ γραφῶν προφητικῶν) in a
passage strikingly akin to our context here, occurring
in the great doxology which closes the Epistle to the
Romans, which in its turn is an echo of Rom. i. 2. Rom. xvi.
Upon this view Eph. iii. 4 loses even the semblance ^{25 f.}
of not being wholly worthy of St Paul.

One other department of evidence alleged to be

---

[1] *Neuhebräisches und chaldäisches Wörterbuch über die Talmudim und Midraschim.* Leipzig, 1876—89.

unfavourable to St Paul's authorship remains to be spoken of, that of language, which falls roughly under three heads, style, phraseology, and vocabulary. As regards style, much stress is laid on the unusually long sentences which meet us in some parts of the Epistle, made up of clauses linked on one to another, often interspersed with more or less parenthetic clauses, and sometimes running into irregular constructions. Thus much is true, and it would not be easy to find exact parallels elsewhere in St Paul's Epistles except in the similar passages of the Epistle to the Colossians and, to a certain extent, in such passages as Rom. i. 1—7; Phil. ii. 5—11; iii. 8—14. But it is difficult to recognise any truth in the allegation that the Epistle to the Ephesians is distinguished by verbosity and unmeaning copiousness of language. On the contrary, within each clause we find the closest packing of · concentrated language, yet all fused together in one glowing stream. The latest and not the least intelligent of recent critics who have found the style of the Epistle un-Pauline has conveniently summed up his impressions on this matter in a single pair of contrasted epithets[1]. The author of the Epistle to the Ephesians betrays, he thinks, a wholly different temperament as a writer from St Paul, a *phlegmatic* instead of a *choleric* temperament. To any one who feels the presence of a phlegmatic temperament in this Epistle, its style,

[1] Von Soden, p. 88.

and a good deal else besides, may well present some
perplexities. The lofty calm which undeniably does
pervade it may in part be due to the mellowing effect
of years, but doubtless much more to the sense of
dangers surmounted, aspirations satisfied, and a van-
tage ground gained for the world-wide harmonious
action of the Christian community under the govern-
ment of God. But, though the vehement moods of the
earlier contests have subsided, many parts of the
Epistle glow with a steady white heat which has to
be taken account of as a considerable factor in the
production of the supposed peculiarities of style.

Another cause of difference is this, that all the
earlier epistles, that to the Romans in part excepted,
are, so to speak, occasional writings, called forth by
special conditions at special times. The Epistle to the
Ephesians, as we have already seen, has on the other
hand a more general character. Time and place are
indeed by no means unimportant as determining
what is to be written, but they are more in the
distance than before. Now for the first time St Paul
is free, as it were, to pour forth his own thoughts in
a positive form, instead of carrying on an argument,
and therefore being hampered by its necessary limitations : and this great change could not but greatly
affect his style in some such manner as we find. It
is true that the Epistle to the Romans was likewise
to a considerable though less extent general in character; but a large proportion of what may be called

general in that Epistle was still either argumentative
or at least expository.   When however, as in some
of its highest flights, it becomes simply affirmative
(see c. i. 1—6, and the last twelve verses of c. viii.,
not to speak of the final Doxology), we are at
once reminded of the Epistle to the Ephesians, alike
by the matter and by the long drawn out style.
Doubtless in those verses of c. viii. the texture, as it
were, is different : the links of the chain are looser :
but essentially the concatenation is there.

The evidence of phraseology and vocabulary is
quite different from that of style, being made up of a
number of separate particulars, which evidently cannot
be dealt with in a complete manner within our
limits.   But it is worth while to speak of some
considerations affecting this class of evidence.   We
will begin with the vocabulary.

Various Introductions supply lists of words found
in Ephesians and not found elsewhere in the Bible,
or found in the LXX., but not elsewhere in the New
Testament.   In these lists it is usual to omit the Pastoral Epistles, or to take account of them separately ;
and with good reason, for evidence derived from them
as to St Paul's own diction would be disputed by the
many critics who on undeniably plausible, though I
believe inadequate, grounds deny their Pauline authorship, such denial being moreover in part founded on
real differences of vocabulary.   But it is an interesting

fact, not without a bearing on the genuineness both of the Epistle to the Ephesians, and of the Pastoral Epistles, that the four have in common a certain number of words not found in the earlier Epistles. But this is by the way, for we must return to the lists intended to illustrate the distinctness of the vocabulary of our Epistle. Lists of this kind are always delusive if taken in a crude numerical fashion. He must be a very monotonous writer indeed who does not use—for the most part unconsciously use—in each of his books a certain number of words which he does not use in his other books : and the same consideration evidently holds good in the comparison with the books of other writers, unless the comparison is made with a considerable mass of writing, and that dealing on the whole with the same class of subjects. Nor again have we any right to expect that the proportion of unique words (unique, I mean, in this limited sense) would be even approximately equal in different works of the same writer : and yet the causes of inequality would be so various, and often so unknown, that we could not expect to be able to account for more than a part of such inequalities as may present themselves. Hence, in such a case as this, the mere counting up of unique words employed is of almost no value : individual words must be looked at one by one.

It ought to be obvious that words occurring only in quotations have no just place in any of these lists. This simple test strikes away 9 out of the 76 words

occurring in one careful enumeration of the words of
this Epistle not used by St Paul elsewhere, the Pastoral Epistles being left out of account. Then a large
part of the list may safely be dismissed from consideration at once because required, or at least
naturally suggested, by contexts which do not recur
Eph. vi.
11—17. in other Epistles. Thus the unique passage on
putting on the panoply of God supplies a number of
words for which there is at least no obvious place in
the earlier Epistles, πανοπλία, βέλος, θυρεός, περιζών-
νυμαι, ὑποδοῦμαι, πάλη, and again two which have a
less obvious place there, κοσμοκράτωρ, ἑτοιμασία. A
few lines later we come to ἐν ἁλύσει, which might at
Eph. vi.
20. first sight be plausibly called a characteristic variation
from St Paul's usual ἐν δεσμοῖς, till we notice the
combination with πρεσβεύω (πρεσβεύω ἐν ἁλύσει),·
shewing that here the writer has in mind not the mere
general thought of being in bonds, but the visual
image of an ambassador standing up to plead his
sovereign's cause and wearing, strangest of contra-
dictions, a fetter by way of official adornment. Of
other words falling under the same head elsewhere
μεσότοιχον, φραγμός, λουτρόν, ὕδωρ, ῥυτίς, σπίλος may
serve as examples. Again the fact that the unity
of the Christian community is so largely dwelt
on accounts at once for a group of words com-
pounded with σύν not found in the other Epistles,
or even in the New Testament, in addition to words
which are found in the other books. Of the former

class are συναρμολογοῦμαι, συνπολίτης, συνοικοδο-
μοῦμαι, σύνσωμος, συνμέτοχος. Somewhat analogous
perhaps are a few cases in which ideas not peculiar to
this Epistle are gathered up in a single unique and
expressive word, as ἐχαρίτωσεν, ἐκληρώθημεν, πολυποίκιλος (ἡ πολυποίκιλος σοφία τοῦ Θεοῦ). Nor can
any weight, as a rule, be attached to words found only
here when St Paul elsewhere uses words differing
only as different parts of speech, the fundamental
meaning being the same. Thus καταρτισμός stands
here alone, but elsewhere we find καταρτίζω and
κατάρτισις; so προσκαρτέρησις, but in other Epistles
προσκαρτερέω, and conversely in reference to the
same subject, prayer, ἀγρυπνέω, but in the Second
Epistle to the Corinthians ἀγρυπνία; ὁσιότης, but
elsewhere ὁσίως; and ἄνοιξις followed by τοῦ στόματος,
but in 2 Cor. vi. 11 the verb ἀνοίγω with τὸ στόμα.
There remain a considerable number of words for the
most part common in all ordinary Greek, the distri-
bution of which in the Epistle to the Ephesians, in
other Epistles of St Paul, in the New Testament, and
in the Septuagint was likely, so far as we can see, to
depend on all kinds of special and accidental causes,
and therefore affords no evidence on the point which
we are considering. One example must be noticed,
because it has attracted an inordinate amount of
attention. In the Epistle to the Ephesians ὁ διάβολος
occurs twice, ὁ Σατανᾶς not at all; whereas St Paul's
earlier Epistles are without ὁ διάβολος, but have ὁ

Σατανᾶς seven times. But in truth this alternative use of the Greek or the Hebrew form is exactly like the alternative use of the Greek or the Hebrew form of St Peter's name within the one Epistle to the Galatians, which has Πέτρος twice and Κηφᾶς four times. Moreover no less than six books of the New Testament, written by four different authors, have both ὁ διάβολος and ὁ Σατανᾶς; viz. St Matthew, St Luke, St John, Acts of the Apostles, First Epistle to Timothy, Apocalypse.

On the other hand no one doubts that the great bulk of the vocabulary of this Epistle is in accordance with Pauline usage, the question at issue being whether its distinctive elements point to a disciple rather than to the master himself. There are a few common words which it is a little surprising to find among the words peculiar to the Epistle to the Ephesians; as ἄγνοια, ἀπατάω, δῶρον, μέγεθος, πρότερος (adjective), φρόνησις: that is, it is a little surprising that St Paul should not have used them elsewhere. But the bare fact that each of these words stands there but once is enough to disqualify them from being taken as marking the style or usage of a different writer. Indeed all this evidence drawn from the mere presence or absence of words on comparison with other books of the same author, or of other authors, can never have much value unless it be copious or very peculiar,—much more so than is the case with respect to this Epistle.

In one small class of words, however, we escape these usually barren calculations and speculations, viz. those words which do occur both in the Epistle to the Ephesians and in earlier Epistles of St Paul, but which are said to be used in a different sense here. Thus it is said that οἰκονομία elsewhere in St Paul's writings (viz. once in 1 Cor. ix. 17 ; for Col. i. 25 is different) denotes St Paul's own stewardship, in this Epistle an ordering of the fulness of the times, or of the grace of God, or of the mystery that had been kept secret. But can there be anything more Pauline than by this use of the same word to point back from the human stewardship to its source and pattern in the divine stewardship? Again περιποίησις in i. 14 is said to be concrete, a special possession, that is to say, a thing specially possessed, whereas elsewhere (viz. once in each epistle to the Thessalonians) it is abstract, 'gaining' or ' acquisition.' The phrase here being confessedly an echo, though not an exact copy, of Old Testament language, the difference at best could weigh little. But in truth there is no difficulty in taking περιποιήσεως in its *prima facie* abstract sense, "unto God's redemption (buying back) of His own special ownership." It would take too long now to discuss the shades of meaning of that extremely difficult word πλήρωμα. For the present it must be enough to say that what seems the most peculiar use of it in this Epistle is, to the best of my belief, a natural extension or

application of a familiar sense of the word not
without example in St Paul, and that the seeming
peculiarity arises from the high and mysterious
nature of the subject to which it is applied.   The
supposed peculiarity in the use of μυστήριον in one
passage of the Epistle to the Ephesians is of a
different kind.   Elsewhere (five times) in this Epistle,
as also in that to the Colossians, it is used for God's
hidden purpose, now at last revealed, to make Himself
known to the Gentiles by the Gospel; this being
merely a natural application of the common meaning
'secret' or 'secret purpose.'   If therefore the sense in
Eph. v. 32 is quite different, there is a difference of
sense within the Epistle itself; and we need not be
greatly surprised if we find that the meaning attached
to the word in this passage differs again from that in
other Epistles of St Paul: particularly as they contain
much variety of application of at least its fundamental
sense.   But in reality the passage gains in force by
the retention of the familiar Pauline sense: the law of
marriage laid down in Genesis as given to Adam was
for St Paul a preliminary indication of a hidden Divine
purpose or ordinance, the full meaning of which was
to be revealed only by the revealing of Christ as the
Head of His spouse the Church.   It would be
only wasting time to consider now half a dozen other
words which on the flimsiest grounds have been added
to those of which I have spoken: they are γενεά,
ποιμήν, πράσσω, σβέννυμι, and the perfect passive of

σώζω; this last being rather a case of supposed doctrinal discrepancy. There remains one word, the use of which is really in a manner unique, ἐπουράνιος, always in the phrase, five times repeated, ἐν τοῖς ἐπουρανίοις. Strictly speaking, however, it is only the phrase that is unique, for there is no definite change of sense in the word itself from 1 Cor. xv. 40, 48, 49 to the first four occurrences of the phrase in the Epistle to the Ephesians. In each of them the association of "the heavenly regions" with the present course of things comes naturally as part of that expansion of the thought of a future world of blessedness into that of a present higher world of blessedness, which we have already had to recognise in this Epistle. What is undeniably perplexing is the use of the same phrase in vi. 12 for the sphere of evil powers; involving the very difficult identification of it with the ἀήρ spoken of in ii. 2, the earthly atmosphere, and giving interest to the fact that the Syriac Version, though probably only by a virtual conjecture, translates as though the reading were ἐν τοῖς ὑπουρανίοις. But this difficulty is irrelevant for our present purpose, the contrasted use of the phrase being in the Epistle itself, not in the earlier Epistles.

Eph. i. 3, 20; ii. 6; iii. 10.

The only remaining point to be spoken of in respect of language is the uniqueness of a certain number of phrases, consisting of several words. The passage we have just been looking at supplies such

Eph. vi. 12. a phrase, τὰ πνευματικὰ τῆς πονηρίας, and the passage
Eph. ii. 2. referred to just before supplies another, τὸν ἄρχοντα
Eph. i. 17. τῆς ἐξουσίας τοῦ ἀέρος; so also we have ὁ πατὴρ τῆς
Eph. iii. δόξης; τὸν πατέρα, ἐξ οὗ πᾶσα πατριὰ ἐν οὐρανοῖς καὶ
15.
Eph. iv.
23. ἐπὶ γῆς ὀνομάζεται; τῷ πνεύματι τοῦ νοὸς ὑμῶν; and
the list might easily be enlarged.   With regard to all
these uniquenesses nothing more need be said than
has been said candidly already by Holtzmann, one of
the most competent of the critics who deny the
genuineness of the Epistle[1]; "all these facts (i.e. such
as we have been now taking note of) "have to be
"recognised, though we may form different judge-
"ments as to their force for purposes of proof.   They
"never stand opposed in direct hostility to St Paul's
"doctrinal views as known from other sources, and
"what occurs for instance in 1 Cor. vi. 3 (οὐκ οἴδατε
"ὅτι ἀγγέλους κρινοῦμεν, μήτιγε βιωτικά;) is not less
"unique."   The fact is that all the evidence from
language supposed to be unfavourable to St Paul's
authorship is pretty generally acknowledged to be
merely accessory and secondary, except that which is
said to be furnished by style, which we have sufficiently examined already.

But it is impossible to leave this part of our

---

[1] *Kritik der Epheser und Kolosser Briefe* (Leipzig, 1872), p. 6.

subject without giving some attention to the special relations between the two Epistles to the Ephesians and to the Colossians, as they play a considerable part in the discussions which have taken place on the genuineness of the former Epistle. The complexity of the problem is attested by the variety of the views held by competent critics. While many accept and many deny the genuineness of both Epistles, others accept that to the Colossians but not that to the Ephesians, and others again hold the Epistle to the Colossians to be partly genuine, partly not.

We have already seen how great likeness there is between the two Epistles, and also how great unlikeness. Much of both the theological and the religious teaching of the Epistle to the Ephesians recurs in that to the Colossians, sometimes in the same or analogous positions, sometimes in different combinations: while on the other hand the latter differs essentially from the former in having a large part of its contents controversial, the points of controversy being specially connected with Judaism though not with the bindingness of the Mosaic Law; and it further differs from our Epistle, as we have already had ample occasion to notice, in the presence of much personal matter in the last twelve verses, not to speak of the opening salutation. But these are only the broader differences. Others not less interesting occur in many of the passages which shew most resemblance.

11—2

The problem being how best to account for the combination of the resemblances and the differences, we may put aside for the moment the solution involved in the supposition that both Epistles are genuine, viz. that they proceeded from the same mind at virtually the same time, and that the intended recipients of the one, while partly surrounded by the same circumstances as the recipients of the other, were also subjected to different influences of which the Apostle took account in writing to them. Nor need we discuss the abstract possibility that the resemblances might be due to use of a common original, dating from a later time than St Paul's life; for that no one, I believe, supposes. If the Epistle to the Ephesians be not genuine, the most obvious suggestion is that it was derived from the Epistle to the Colossians, whether that itself be genuine or not. The generality of the language of the Epistle to the Ephesians gives it an unusual look; while that to the Colossians in form is more like St Paul's other epistles; and the concrete shape taken by its controversial matter has a more obviously historical appearance than anything in the Epistle to the Ephesians.

But when critics have tried to work out the problem in detail, they have found it by no means so simple as it appeared at first: for if on a broad view the Epistle to the Colossians has the look of greater originality, a closer study sometimes suggests the opposite conclusion. When Holtzmann had worked out the comparison with endless pains, the result he arrived at was that the Epistle to the Ephesians was written near the end of the first century, with various borrowings from an Epistle to Colossians, not however from our Epistle to the Colossians at full length as it stands, but from a much shorter Epistle now imbedded in ours, and then that this shorter Epistle was lengthened out by the author of the Epistle to the Ephesians, with interpolations in imitation of his own work. Truly an extraordinary process, not to be thought credible without very clear evidence indeed, and leaving inexplicable the most characteristic differences between the two Epistles in those doctrinal passages which they have in common.

The only key to the intricacies of this variously reciprocal appearance of originality is the ordinary supposition that both Epistles have throughout one author, who in the corresponding parts of both was setting forth the same leading ideas, needing to be modified in range and proportion in accordance with special circumstances, and to be variously clothed in language accordingly. In such a case we can hardly speak of one being prior to the other: both would or might be products of the same short space of time and the same state of mind. If the needs of the Colossians called for controversial or negative warnings against special dangers, yet these warnings equally needed as a positive base some kind of repetition of the doctrinal matter so prominent in the

Epistle to the Ephesians. An excellent example for study may be borrowed from Holtzmann[1]. If we put together Eph. iii. 8 f. and 16 f., and then again Eph. i. 9 and 18; and then compare these two combinations of passages together, and each with Col. i. 27, we shall find a striking series of coincidences with different surroundings. The several passages of the Epistle to the Ephesians might be described as in one sense expansions of parts of the single longer passage of that to the Colossians in different directions: but the coincident phrases in the two Epistles are as much at home, as it were, in their respective contexts in the one Epistle as in the other.

Attention has been called to the undeniable fact that the prayer in Eph. i. 18 ff. is for knowledge, that the recipients of the Epistle may " know what is the hope of God's calling, and what the riches of the glory of His inheritance among the Saints "; while the corresponding prayer in Col. i. 10 is for godly living, that the Colossians may " walk worthily of the Lord unto all pleasing, in every good work bearing fruit." But this apparent contrast, when closely examined, will be found to be only a matter of local proportion. The prayer in the former Epistle has a no less practical goal in view than the prayer in the latter. Besides Eph. ii. 1—3 and the last half of the Epistle, it is well to note ii. 10, in which God's purpose

---

[1] *Einleitung in das Neue Testament*, 3te Auflage (Freiburg i. B., 1892), p. 263.

in making and redeeming man is expressly described,
"for we are His workmanship (ποίημα), created in
"Christ Jesus for good works which God afore pre-
"pared that we should walk in them." And again
conversely the prayer for the Colossians begins
almost in the same terms as the other prayer, "that Col. i. 9.
ye may be filled with the knowledge of His will in all
wisdom and spiritual understanding"; and in the
next verse continues thus the words just cited above,
"in every good work bearing fruit and growing *by
the knowledge of God.*"

Again the idea of the Church as the Body of
which the Christ is the Head is practically the same in
Col. ii. 19 as it is in Eph. iv. 15 f. But the idea of
membership, which in the Epistle to the Colossians
is only implied, is worked out fully for the Ephesians,
and thus gives rise to an important section of our
Epistle. Every one must feel how fit the exposition
of this membership would be for an epistle to the
churches of Proconsular Asia, in which high morality
and religion were to be set forth in their true relation
to high theology.

The more closely we scrutinise those parts of both
Epistles which most nearly resemble each other,—
scrutinise them comparatively and scrutinise them in
their respective contexts,—the less possible it becomes
to find traces of a second-hand imitative character
about the language of either. The stamp of freshness
and originality is on both; and thus the subtle

intricacies of likeness and unlikeness of language are a peculiarly strong kind of evidence for identical authorship, whether the author be St Paul or another. Whatever therefore supports the genuineness or the lateness of either Epistle does the same for the other. Hence the evidence for the Epistle to the Colossians becomes indirect evidence for the Epistle to the Ephesians. It would take us too long to examine separately the evidence respecting the former Epistle, beyond what we have already had occasion to consider in respect of personal and geographical details. In the latter we have found no tangible evidence against St Paul's authorship, and so it would be also if we examined the Epistle to the Colossians in the same manner. In both we have not merely the *prima facie* evidence of his name in the text and in unanimous ancient tradition, but close and yet for the most part not superficial connexion in language with his other Epistles, and that not such a connexion as can with any reasonable probability be explained by the supposition of borrowing. Above all, we find in both the impress of that wondrous heart and mind.

A few words must suffice on the relation of the Epistle to the Ephesians to the First Epistle of St Peter. Their affinity has been often noticed of late years, and comes the more clearly to light the more attentively each is studied. Opinion is much divided as to relative priority. One ingenious critic, Seufert[1], who has traced out many not obvious coincidences, besides imagining others, comes to the conclusion that both Epistles were written by the same author, and that he lived in the second century. The truth is that in the First Epistle of St Peter many thoughts are derived from the Epistle to the Ephesians, as others are from that to the Romans: but St Peter makes them fully his own by the form into which he casts them, a form for the most part unlike what we find in any epistle of St Paul's.

[1] In Hilgenfeld's *Zeitschrift für wissenschaftliche Theologie*, Leipzig, 1881, pp. 178, 332.

IV.

THE PURPOSE OF THE EPISTLE.

WE come now to the purpose of the Epistle as related to St Paul's own life and work. On this subject it will not be possible for me to avoid some repetitions (in other words) of what I have had to say more than once before in connexion with different epistles or different aspects of the apostolic age. Our Epistle is the worthy fruit of the culmination of St Paul's career; but to understand it in this light, we must have some perception of the steps which led up to it.

Every one knows that St Paul's career as an apostle was determined by the part which he took with reference to the great question of his day, the relation of Jew to Gentile within the Church. But it needs some reflexion to gain a clear sense of the variety of the issues which were included within that one comprehensive question, and which had to be dealt with in one way or another by this Jewish Apostle to the Gentiles. The Bible gives no support

to the common notion that there were two true "re-
ligions," as they are conventionally called, the Jewish
and the Christian, the one ending at the moment
when the other began.   The fundamental change
brought by the coming of Christ was a deepening and
enlargement of the one imperishable faith in the Lord
God of Israel, and this change included gradations in
its own accomplishment, and also in the manner in
which it affected different classes of men.   The
interval between the Resurrection and the Fall of
Jerusalem was for Jewish Christians subject to wholly
different conditions from the later time when the holy
place was visibly forsaken.   Then again the differences of conditions affecting Jews of the Dispersion
on the one hand and Jews of Palestine on the other,
would naturally affect Jewish Christians of the Dispersion and of Palestine in the same manner; while
Gentile Christians would of course be differently
situated from both.   St Paul himself shared the conditions of both the first two of· these three classes.
He was born a Jew of the Cilician Dispersion : he
was brought up a Jew of the strictest Palestinian
education.   Then, having become above all men
identified with the third class, having been Divinely
appointed to be the foremost herald of the Gospel to
the Gentiles, and constrained by Jewish and Judaistic
exclusiveness to become the champion of the freedom
of Gentile Christians from Jewish law, he had to steer
a difficult way in his own person and in his teaching

and administration; resisting sternly where resistance
was needed, but in all things striving to build up, and
to avoid whatsoever might have the effect of pulling
down.

So far as we form our impression of St Paul from
his own writings, we naturally form it predominantly
from those writings which are fullest of personal
action, and openly displayed feeling, and eager main-
tenance of a cause. These are the four Epistles of the
second group, belonging to the time when the contest
with the Judaizers had still to be carried on in Asia
Minor and Greece, to say the least. Holding as he
did that the true nature of the Gospel would be
incurably falsified if once it were to be allowed that
Gentile converts must be circumcised and keep other
precepts of the Jewish ceremonial law in order to
be admitted to full fellowship as Christians, it was
impossible that his writings of this period should not
bear that particular colour. This is of course specially
true of the Epistle to the Galatians, which had this
contention for its primary subject. But it is a great
mistake to suppose that the particular battle which
had just then to be fought is by itself a sufficient
key to all his policy, if we may so call it, and all his
aspiration. A baseless assumption to this effect is the
main cause of the suspicion which rises in the minds
of many critics when they read in the Acts various
sayings and doings ascribed to him, which shew a
conciliatory and more than conciliatory behaviour

towards Jewish Christianity in Jewish Christians. But the fact is, that conciliatory behaviour finds ample justification in the mental attitude implied in much of the Epistle to the Romans, and contradicted by nothing even in the Epistle to the Galatians or in the second to the Corinthians. The clear and decided manner in which in writing to the Romans he upholds the unique positions assigned by the Lord of the Ages to the ancient Israel in the revelation and the salvation which He prepared for all mankind in His Son Jesus, is in entire accordance with the sleepless anxiety with which he laboured to avert a severance between the original Palestinian Church of Jewish Christians, and the daily multiplying and expanding churches of Gentile Christians.

The anxiously devised external expression of this desire was (1) that collection made in Gentile churches for the poor Christians of Palestine which so puzzles and perhaps wearies modern readers, for it fills a considerable place in the Acts and Epistles ; and (2) the carrying of this collection to Jerusalem by himself in person as the recognised head of Gentile Christianity. Nor was this a mere piece of ceremonious ambassadorship. The carrying of that offering to Jerusalem meant the carrying of his own life ready to be offered as the most sacred oblation of all. He knew with what deadly hatred the unbelieving Jews hated him, how eagerly they would seize on the opportunity of wreaking it upon him if

he shewed himself in Jerusalem, and how small his
chance of escape would be. The deliberate way
in which he faced this prospect shews the transcendent
importance which he attached to the act, an act
which would, he trusted, bear its desired fruit whether
he lived or died, for his death in such a cause would
be the mightiest of influences to bind together the
Jewish and Gentile churches.

But he knew also that it might be God's good
pleasure to preserve him from imminent death once
more, and in that case he looked forward to being
the instrument for the further carrying out of the
purpose of his perilous mission in another way, viz.
by pausing on his westward journey back from
Jerusalem to make a stay at Rome. The purpose
is expressed in Acts xix. 21, at the very beginning of
the circuitous journey by which he was to reach
Jerusalem, at the end of the long stay at Ephesus.
How much all this meant to him we may gather
by a little reading between the lines in the last twenty
verses of Rom. xv., written not long after, full as they
are of reticences and half-utterances. He was not
going to Rome to found a church: the Roman Church
had long been there already, founded by we know not
whom, or rather more probably of half-spontaneous
growth. He wrote to the Roman Christians with
Rom. xv. careful avoidance of an authoritative tone, yet some-
15. what boldly, he says, in part as by way of reminding
them of truths in some sense already known, on

the strength of the special "grace" (divine office) divinely assigned to him in relation to the Gentiles. It was a delicate and peculiar position, anxious as he was to hold rigorously to his principle of not building on a foundation laid by other men; but he evidently felt that, if he lived, it was of great consequence for unity that he should set foot himself in Rome, and thus establish in his own person a living bond of fellowship between the churches of his own founding and the remote churches of Judea on the one hand, and on the other this independently founded church, which was also the church of the capital of the empire or civilised world. Such thoughts probably had had a share in his long-standing desire to visit Rome, but now they received a double consecration by his purposed carrying of the Gentile offering to Jerusalem. If he were permitted to accomplish this, and thus set the seal for the Gentile Christians on this fruit of his labour and of their love, he knew that in coming to the Romans he would be coming with what he calls a fulfilment of blessing from Christ. The victory of peace won in Jerusalem would be celebrated with restful fellowship (συναναπαύσωμαι ὑμῖν) in central Rome itself; and this concurrence of circumstances would be of bright omen for the future. Rom. xv. 28.

Rom. xv. 29.

Rom. xv. 32.

We have already seen, in part, how much there is in the Epistle to the Romans itself in harmony with this aspiration. Its first chapters place Jew and

Gentile on a level as regards their failure in the past, and their admission to Christian faith in the present;—on a level, yet two or three times with indication of a certain priority though not superiority of the Jew (ʼΙουδαίῳ τε πρῶτον καὶ ῞Ελληνι). In the ninth, tenth, and eleventh chapters, starting from his own anguish at the thought of God's seeming rejection of His own people, he carries back their very unbelief to the purpose of God; refuses to allow that the admission of the Gentiles involves God's casting away of His people whom He foreknew; treats the admission of the Gentiles, on the ground of mercy, simply as a grafting into the one ancient olive tree, at the same time warning them against contempt for the natural branches; and sets forth the future triumph of mercy in the recovery of unbelieving Israel out of unbelief. Again the peace and unity of Jew and Gentile is evidently the leading thought in that exhortation to being of the same mind one with another and with one accord glorifying God with one mouth, which winds up the elaborate inculcation of mutual forbearance in matters of conscience in the fourteenth chapter; ending with fresh quotations from the Old Testament, all in various ways suggesting the idea, which in one of them is clearly expressed, " Rejoice, ye nations, with His people."

These were St Paul's thoughts when he was writing to Rome, with hope and desire to visit Rome at the end of his perilous mission undertaken in the same

cause, if only he should return from it alive. The
Epistle to the Ephesians springs mainly from the
same thoughts at a later point in the marvellous
drama, itself written from Rome to those churches of
Western Asia Minor in which he had been spending
the years preceding his start for Jerusalem by way of
Greece. Nothing was more natural than that under
these circumstances, in sending Tychicus to commu-
nicate in person with these churches, he should send
by his hand a written epistle, which should combine at
once the lessons most needed to be spoken to them
at that time and the long cherished thoughts of his own
meditation. In so writing to these churches he may
well have felt at the same time that he was virtually
speaking through them to all Gentile Christendom, and
leaving in this Epistle the true and sufficient completion, as it were, of his earlier teaching of the Gentiles.
Anticipation had now been turned into fulfilment. He
had borne the Gentile offering to Jerusalem, seen it
accepted by James and the Jewish Church, escaped
the clearly foreseen peril of death only by the Roman
governor's interference. Not as a free traveller, but
as a Roman prisoner, having appealed to Caesar as
a Roman citizen, he had reached Rome more than
two years later than he hoped, and had a singular
opportunity to preach in his own person in the capital
of the world. He had proposed to himself to pay
the Christian community of Rome a passing visit
for mutual encouragement: but now the hand of God

had manifestly set him down in Rome as a new home, such as first Antioch and then Ephesus had been, and, lying chained in the hired lodging which served as his prison, he was free to exhort and instruct every one who came in to him. To what cities or lands the Gospel had been carried during his imprisonment, we do not know; but that matters little. The universality designed by God for the Gospel and for the society of believers in the Gospel must have come home to him with quite new power and with a new pledge of assured victory, when after a long series of labours from province to province he found himself thus wonderfully placed in the earthly centre of earthly universality among men. Some find the sign of another authorship than St Paul's in the sense of accomplished progress looked back upon, which breathes in our Epistle. But this is just the sense which would now at last be naturally justified in a way that it could not be when any of the earlier Epistles were written. Thus at once the course of outward events, and the ripening of the thoughts which we know to have been in his mind when his long stay at Ephesus had come to an end, will fully account both for the universality which is the special note of the Epistle, and for the practical purpose in which the universality of Christian fellowship is embodied, the unity and peace of Jew and Gentile as Christians. In an earlier lecture[1] we had occasion

[1] See pages 125 ff.

for other purposes to consider the three principal passages in which the two elements of the one society are most clearly distinguished for this purpose, i. 12, 13 ; ii. 1—6 ; and the whole section ii. 11—22. The last clause of ii. 15 especially deserves notice, " that He may create (found) in Himself the two into one new man, making peace." It conducts us from the two peoples who are so prominent in the Epistle to the Romans to the one people, or one man, which in that Epistle is nowhere explicitly set forth, though it is implied in its teachings and aspirations, and indeed in that image of the olive tree, but now in the Epistle to the Ephesians is to be brought into clear prominence.

This idea then of the unity of Christians as forming a single society with Christ for its invisible Head, which in different forms dominates the whole Epistle, was the natural outflow of the Apostle's mind at this time, as determined by the course of outward and inward history on the basis of his primary faith. It was needed to be set forth for the completion of his Gospel. On the other hand it was equally needed for the instruction of the no longer infant churches of Western Asia Minor, in whom the Greek spirit of separateness and independence was doubtless working with dangerous vigour.

We have already had occasion to trace some of the anticipations of the more fully developed doctrinal contents of our Epistle which may be discerned in the

earlier Epistles. But, apart from details, the mere fact that it carries us (and that in common with the Epistle to the Colossians) to heights and depths of theology before unvisited deserves special attention in connexion both with St Paul's own life and with the needs of those for whom he wrote. One clause of that Epistle puts before us his leading thought in
Col. ii. 3. this matter, " Christ, in whom are all the treasures of wisdom and knowledge hidden." The first two or three chapters of the First Epistle to the Corinthians are very instructive here. While thanking God that those keen-witted Greek Christians of Corinth had
1 Cor. i. 5. been " enriched in Christ Jesus, in all speech and all knowledge," he is careful to rebuke their pride of wisdom and to let them know how little capable of the highest wisdom he thought them as yet. In teaching them he had rigorously limited himself to
1 Cor. ii. the simplest form of the Gospel, " Jesus Christ and
2, iii. 1, 2. Him crucified," because they had been, nay and were still, but babes in Christ, fit to be fed with milk only, not with the food of full-grown men. While, however, he had thus abstained in his preaching to them from setting forth wisdom, he desired them to know that he possessed a wisdom which he spoke among
1 Cor. ii. the perfect, the full-grown (τοῖς τελείοις), " a wisdom
6, 7. of God in a mystery, the hidden wisdom, which God foreordained before the ages unto our glory." Here then, and elsewhere in the passage, we have clear evidence that Paul had already in his own mind

what he called a wisdom, which as yet he dared
not impart to his still immature converts. But if
so, it was but natural that he should desire in due
time to find a right opportunity for making known
what he believed to have been thus revealed to him.
Various signs shew that this wisdom, as he understood
it, was founded on the recognition of the wisdom of
God Himself, and that the wisdom of God Himself
was in St Paul's mind mainly associated with what
he called the "mystery," the mighty plan of God
running through the ages, according to which He
used unbelief and rejection of Himself for His own
purposes till the appointed time was come and Jesus
Christ was born. Accordingly in the burst of praise cp. 1 Cor.
which crowns his setting forth of the universality ^{i. 21.}
of God's mercy in the future, at the end of Rom. xi.,
(" For God shut up all [τοὺς πάντας, Jews and Gentiles
alike] into disobedience that He might have mercy
upon all "), he dwells on the depth of the riches (i.e.
resourcefulness) and *wisdom and knowledge* of God;
and in the same sense the doxology which ends
the Epistle to the Romans is addressed to the only
wise God. And precisely the same thought recurs
in that phrase of the Epistle to the Ephesians
which has already come before us " the πολυποίκιλος Eph. iii.
wisdom of God." 10.

But the Christian wisdom, which thus rested on a
true perception of God's own wisdom in His ordering
of the ages, carried with it those high thoughts

respecting Christ which are set forth in the Epistles to the Ephesians and the Colossians. It was an interpretation of human history and experience in the light of the Cross and the Resurrection: but what gave the interpretation its force for men whose reflexions went deeper than the elements of simple faith was the perception of Christ's Headship as universal in all worlds and as coeval with creation, and of all His work in those last days as being a fulfilment of what had in some sense been from the beginning.

This was the Christian wisdom and knowledge at its highest. But no less characteristic of our Epistle and that to the Colossians is the stress laid on wisdom and knowledge in a wider sense, as needed for Christian life and progress. In the earliest years of Christian communities other requirements must naturally take precedence. But when the first fervour had begun to chill, and at the same time increasing numbers and increasing complexity of community life had raised new questions, practical and theoretical, it became specially needful to dwell on the need of wisdom, first for fresher and fuller knowledge of what was contained in the Christian faith itself, and then for discernment of what it involved for the guidance of social and personal life. The new Christian faith stood alone in the absoluteness of its requirement of wisdom, though the religious importance of wisdom was not unknown to either the later Jews or the later Greeks and

Romans. But neither Christ nor the Apostles gave a Law to replace for Gentile Christians the Mosaic Law, much less any substitute for the traditions of the elders. In its place were given the historical Gospel and the ever-living Spirit to draw out the significance of its teaching, as need after need should arise : and the preparation on the human side for the apprehension of such teaching of the Spirit was wisdom. Well then might St Paul's language, when he was writing to these Churches, overflow with his sense of the peculiar necessity of wisdom to make all other gifts available for them even now, and much more in the future, when even his remote guidance should have passed away.

The only other point which it is now needful to mention with regard to the Purpose of the Epistle is one to which I had to refer in speaking of St Paul's special motive for his repeated and emphatic references to his own divine mission to the Gentiles, and the imprisonments and other sufferings which he had undergone on this account. It was to give weight to his warnings against lowering the Christian standard of morals and religion by acquiescence in traditional heathen maxims and ways. It is easy to see how, when the first fresh ardour of Christian discipleship had passed away, the inherited and ingrained habits and instincts would unawares resume a partial sway, cp. 1 Pet. i. 14—18, and by the help of plausible excuses a baser type of 22; ii. 1— Christianity would insensibly arise. This lowering of 3, 11, 16; iv. 3.

standard would chiefly take two forms, (1) a self-asserting individualism, injurious to love, fellowship and subjection ; and (2) a dangerous indulgence towards breaches of purity.

These indications must suffice respecting the general purpose of the Epistle.

* * * * * * *

ABSTRACT OF LECTURES.

[BEGUN MICHAELMAS TERM, 1890.]

I. RECIPIENTS.

III. AUTHORSHIP.

i. *External Evidence.*

CAMBRIDGE: PRINTED BY J. AND C. F. CLAY, AT THE UNIVERSITY PRESS.

For EU product safety concerns, contact us at Calle de José Abascal, 56–1°, 28003 Madrid, Spain or eugpsr@cambridge.org.